THE DIAGNOSIS SHOULD HAVE BEEN ARTIST

SYLVIANN MURRAY

ART AND POETRY
"BIPOLAR-CREATIVE"

EDITED BY ALICE BATT AND COLIN MALINAK
COVER DESIGN BY CATHERINE CLEARY

Acknowledgements

Thank you, Alice Batt.
Without your help, this book would never have existed.

-SA Murray

First Published: 2014

ISBN-13: 978-1499652680

Published by SylviAnn Murray
P.O. Box 302528
Austin, TX 78703

Cover design by Catherine Cleary
Cover art, "Cosmic Child," by SylviAnn Murray
Back cover art, "Rainbow Tiger," by SylviAnn Murray
SAMurrayART.com

Dedicated to all my peers at Austin Clubhouse, who feel like family to me.

Introductions to Madness

Madness… creativity. Madness, insanity,
losing one's mind. Going "over the edge."
Frightening, few return, few rebuild.

Finding myself a prisoner, a white room,
stripped of clothing, no dignity. Finding
myself an animal, knowing they are watching
as I bounce off the padded walls, raging,
anger that cannot be released, so much anger
going back to the first unjust confinement,
going back to the first white room…
going back to the child, the crime I don't
remember. Too vividly, too insane.
Losing my mind. Going back… losing my head.

Released to drugs, straps, bindings… I
protest too loudly that I am not insane.
To no avail. No one believes me. I labor
under the belief that I do not belong here
with the other zombies who have given up and
accepted their fate, resigned to a half life
locked away or playing quietly society's game.
They bought the crap they have been spoonfed.
They have become the illness and no longer
resist its deathly lure.

Yes, the different will be condemned. Protected
from their craziness, bizarre creative
urges, their strange compulsions, the knowledge
they are not supposed to have. Thorazine
suppresses it, other drugs… overmedication
to compliance.

Who will believe me? I am in a locked ward,
a psychiatric ward. I am labeled in a rather
terminal way… "Manic-Depressive Disorder."
I am not a person, calling on the pay phone,
who will believe I don't belong here?

I soon learn to behave because it's easier than seclusion, or restraints, or thorazine. We all learn to behave and not reveal how suicidal this place makes us. We all learn that there is no chance of ending it all in this eternal hell-hole. No relief here.

The only hope is to convince "them" especially the doctor with the silver rimmed glasses and the notebook, that we are all "OK" now thanks to all this "help" we have been forced to receive.

I know that my soul has been executed, once again. I need some semblance of freedom from this insane asylum to rebuild what has been killed.

Looking back…

Between the ages of 17 and 30 I was locked up against my will 14 different times. Usually the stays were short as I was not a "good patient" and ESCAPED. But the damage was done quickly in even the most exclusive psychiatric wards.

It has taken me much too long to find out I am an Artist (in 1990 after moving to Austin). Too much of my life has been wasted recovering from "help" I was forced to receive, shedding stigmatizing labels, and breaking free from mind sets passed down from parents who saw creativity as sickness or silly.

My conclusion:
The DIAGNOSIS should have been: ARTIST

SylviAnn Murray, 2013

A Few Words from an Admirer

I met SylviAnn while I was serving on the board at Austin Clubhouse and teaching a class on nonprofit writing at The University of Texas at Austin. My students were doing a story-telling project that semester, and SylviAnn agreed to let Colin Malinak, a senior at the time, compile some of her poems and artwork into a book. After the semester ended, SylviAnn and I worked together to expand the book to include a broader range of her work. Another student from class, Catherine Cleary, designed the cover. The result of our combined efforts is this volume, which depicts with clarity, richness, and raw honesty the challenges of living with mental illness, and the confusion, excitement, terror, and beauty of living true to one's unique creative vision.

SylviAnn, I am a huge fan of you and your work. Thank you for sharing your artistry and your soul with the world, with my students, and with me.

Alice Batt, Ph.D.

Table of Contents

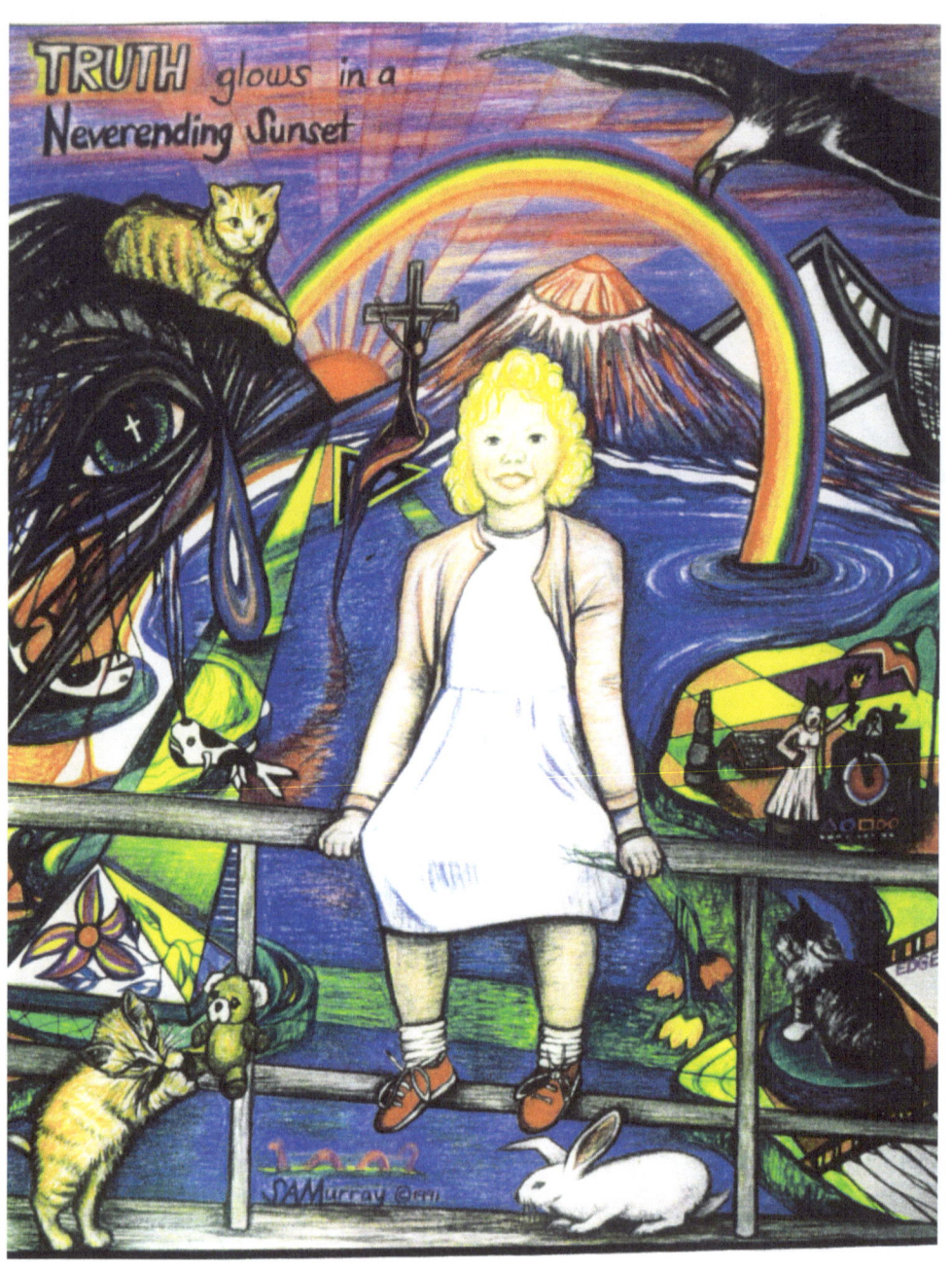

Truth Glows

Too Much Stuff

I have too much STUFF
   too much STUFF
It's scary when it starts coming out
every time I open my mouth to speak
or pick up a pen
   to write   to draw

too much STUFF
   but I have it
and to survive
I have stuffed it
   killed it
   ate it
   and spat it out

Now it is on the walls
of your favorite night spot
I have covered the white walls
   with EMOTION
that would not stay stuffed
   any longer
with FEELING that fell
screaming out of this brain
that IMPLODED
   so many years
that stuffed it
   so many years
Now EXPLODING
   outward
is the only way
   to SURVIVE

Bright colors
fighting creatures
Images
   from other times
I am not responsible for them
but I did find the paper
   and the colors
that was hard enough
I did hold myself down
   in one space
to let it all come out
I did release my own chains
   one by one
to allow subconscious
SCREAMS
to emerge
to build
to come forth
I have put my S O U L
on the white and yellow walls
I A M A L I V E
if you will take the time
to stop and look
I D I D S U R V I V E
and I A M here now seeking
Humanity
who need to cover walls of black
of white
to cover empty walls
from many years of pushing the
colors inside
I am here...Are you A L I V E?

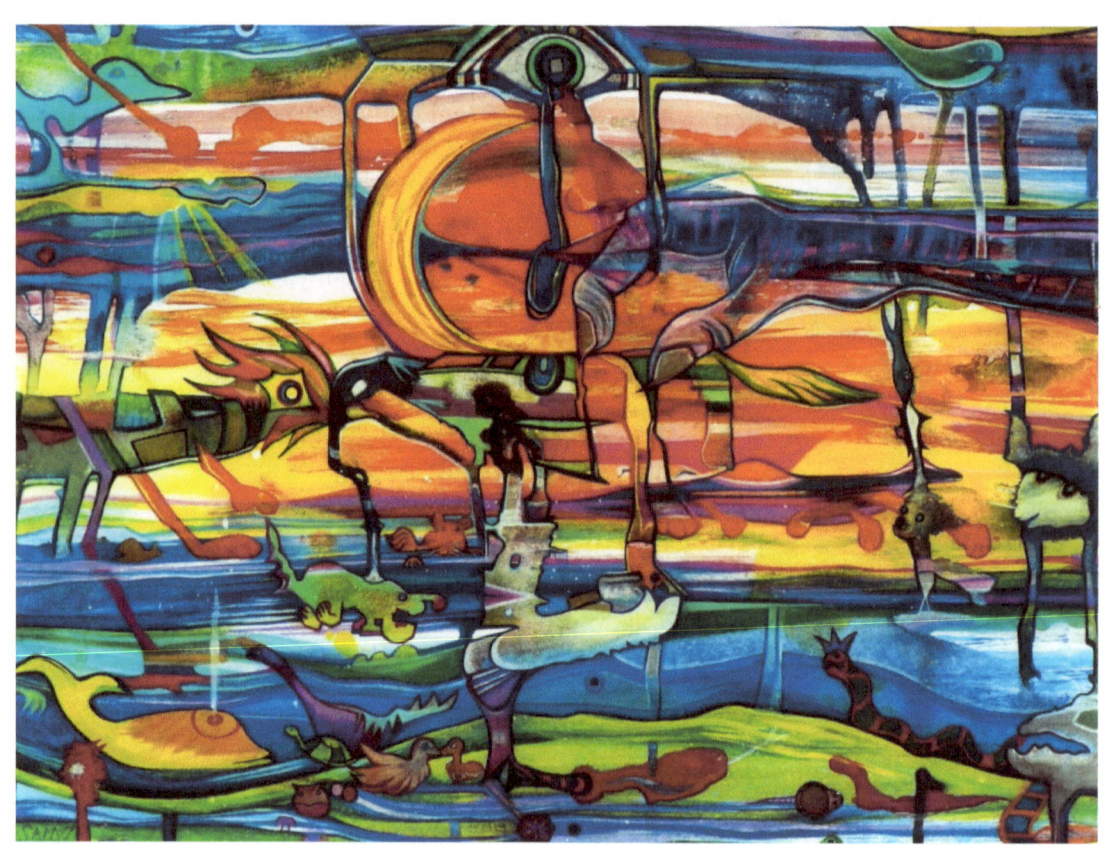

8th Meditation

When Birds Go Crazy

What does it mean
when the birds
go on strike
gather randomly
instead of orderly
flying south
but sideways
and upside down

I feel a sense of excitement
as BLACK BIRDS
fly low and like missiles
almost almost
hit my white ART jeep

I look for feathers
on the pavement
and wonder aloud
why the birds
fly SO low
and in such a chaotic manner
as if the world might suddenly
come to an end...

Are they ALL suicidal
like I recently was
or are they simply
flying close to the ground
searching for food?

sometimes flying
in a homicidal rage
into windows
or smashing
onto pavement
that should have been
a forest or park

But always I know
that it all means so much
and only the birds (as a whole)
black beady eyes
KNOW why

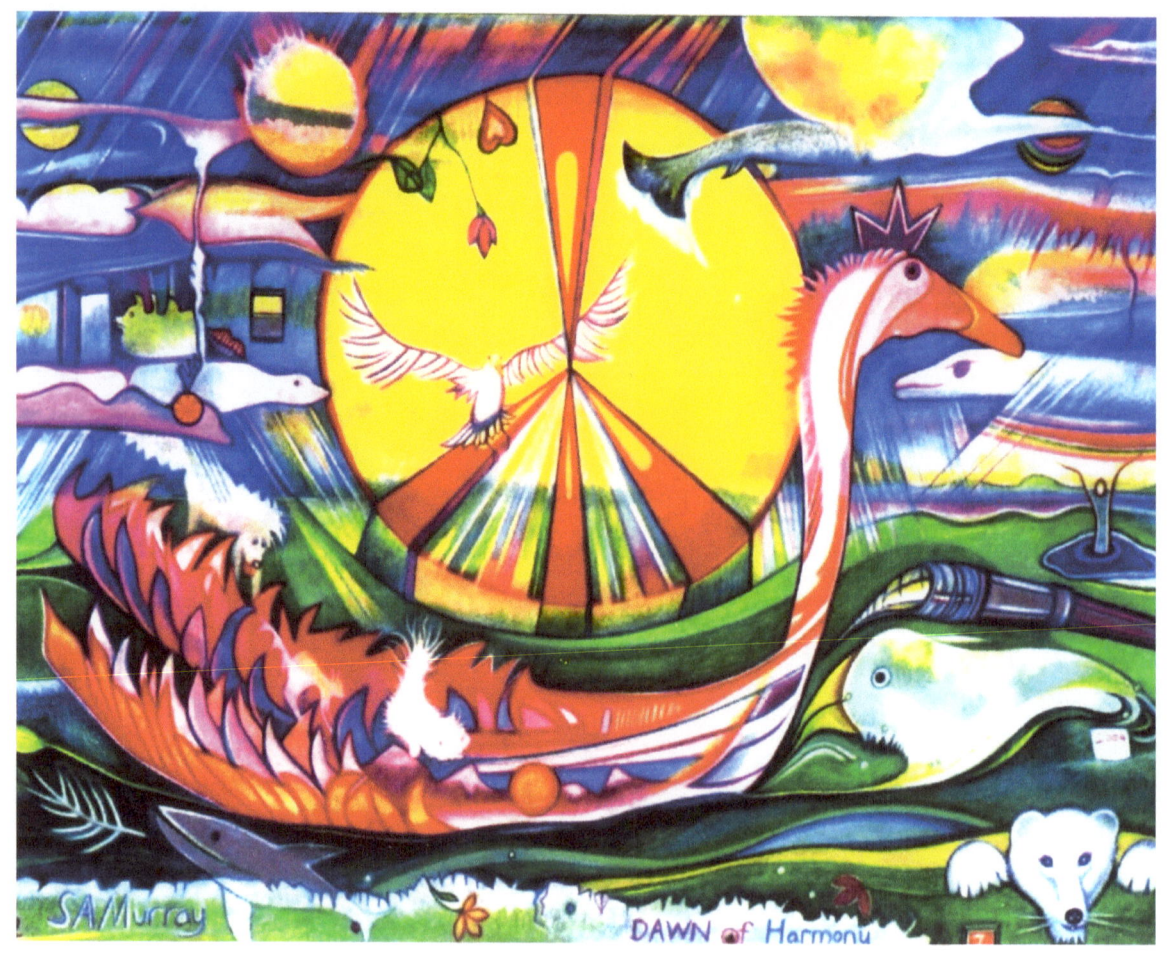

Dawn of Peace

Into The Blue

stop   stop
I want to   get off

I find   my self
at the   door step
to the   stop
and   yes   I   want
to   get   off

I   fall   quickly
in to   the   abyss
and   lose   time
to the   Other   Side

Who   am   I
when   I   emerge
up side   down
for get ting   where   I   was

won der ing   how   I   came
to fall   in to   the   BLUE
to   land   smack
upon   the   chess board
to be   the Queen   be head ed
switched   at the last   minute

I   will be   the castle   now
with   end less   BLUE Streams
running   amuck
through   centuries old   oak trees

I   will   sedately   glance
at   Blue   SKIES
and   find   my self
at   once
the   Blue ness
of my EYES

the M A N I C rainbow

First time I flew
The M A N I C rainbow

I told the world every thing
I knew I could BE
and thought I already WAS
though no one could see

Declared me "CRAZY"
for believing in my self
t o o   m u c h

Tied me down
left me ALONE
to d e s p a i r

Convicted me of a   "crime"
called   IN SANITY

They said
"There is NO RETURN"

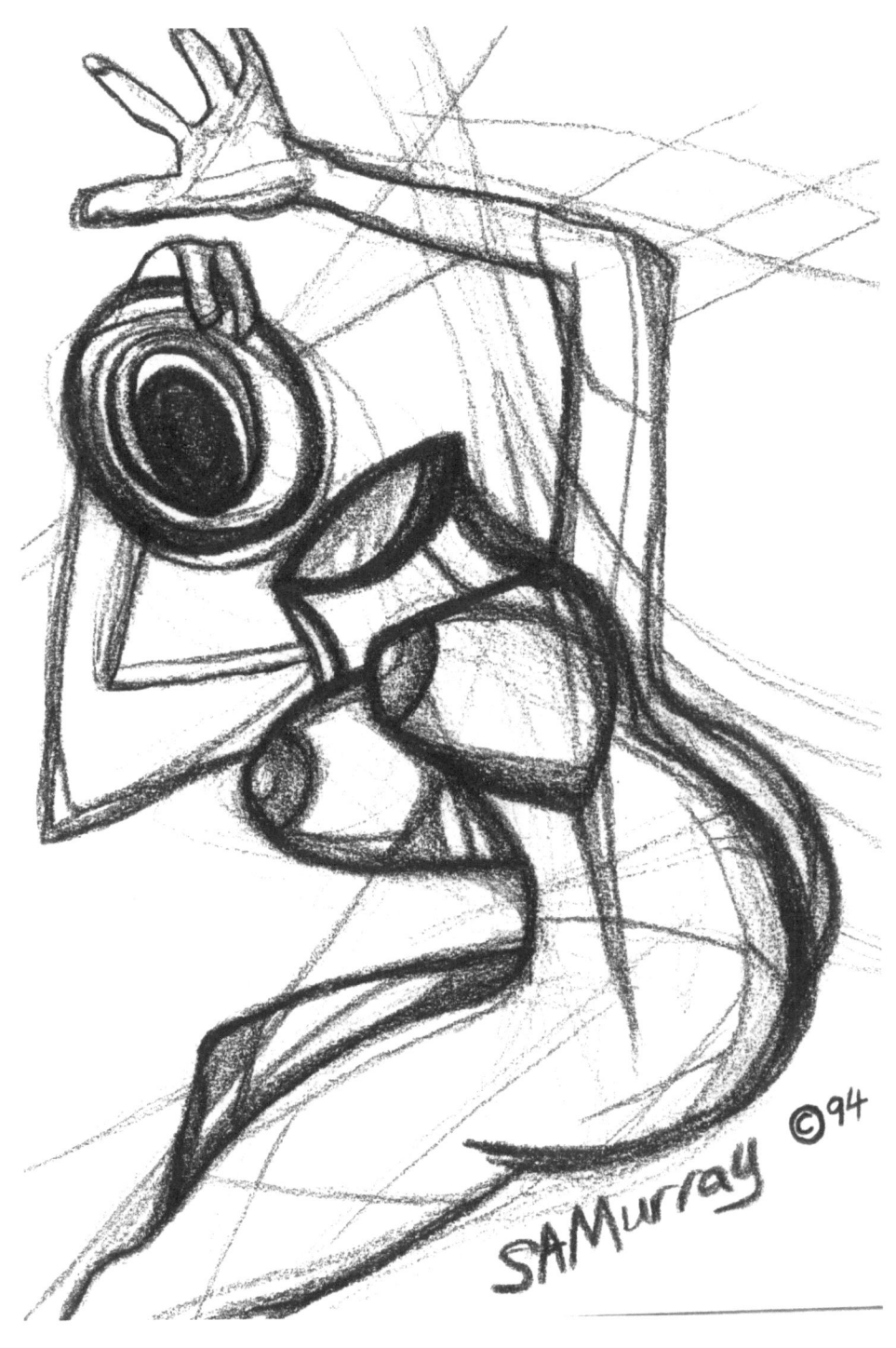

Losing My Head

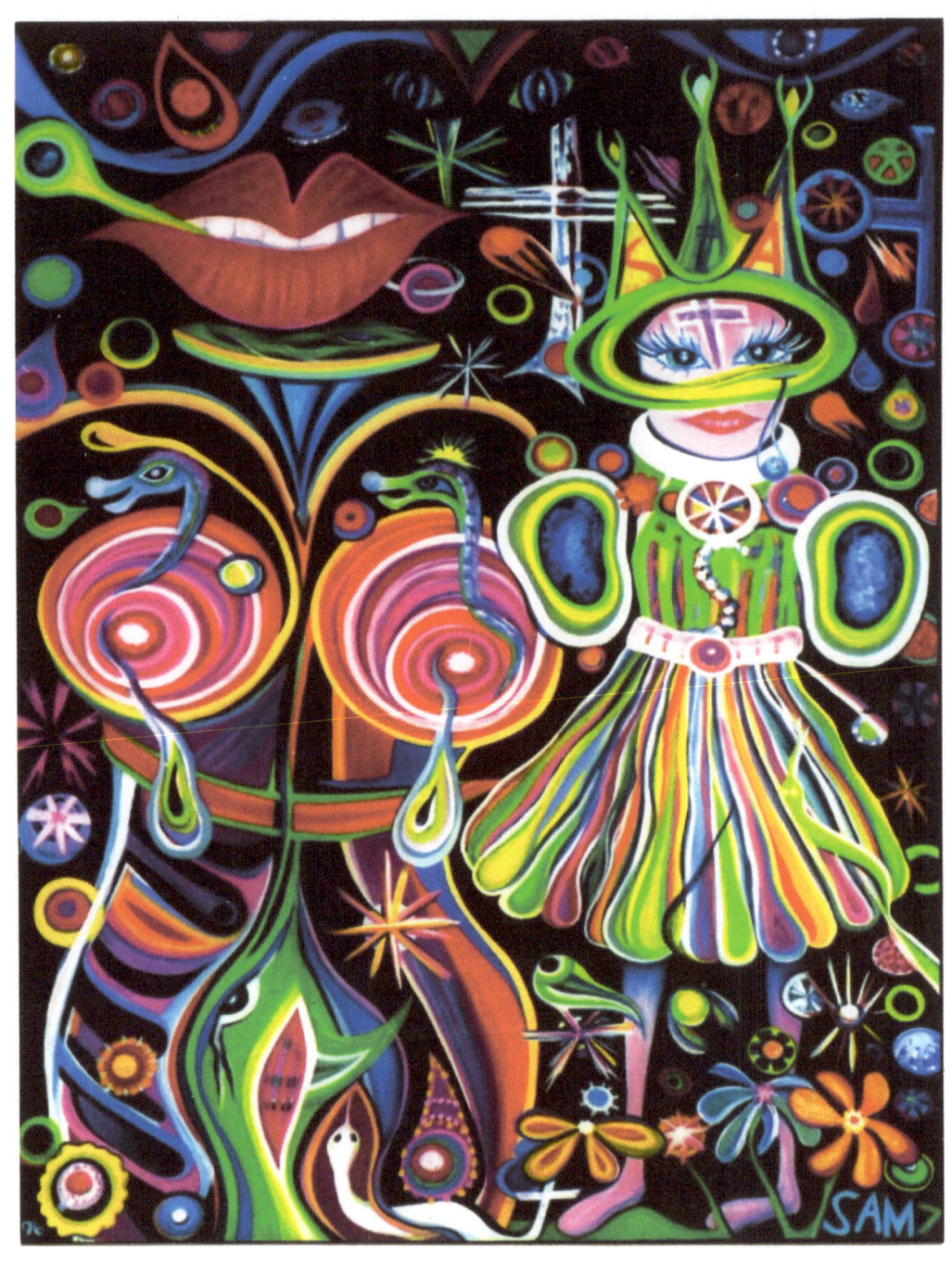

Cosmic Child

Cosmic Interpreter

Life has no ground rules
for an Artist

my life is a mission
I don't have the answers
to the whys
they are inside
a Soul Universal

a few can access
open minds   blue eyes
feel the tug   and respond

I am a Cosmic Interpreter
speaking a language Universal
no words   only images

the answers   the contradictions
reality   insanity
the feelings are mine
yours   everywhere

I put them down
you tell me
what they mean

Art is a Universal Language
the answers are there
You are the interpreter

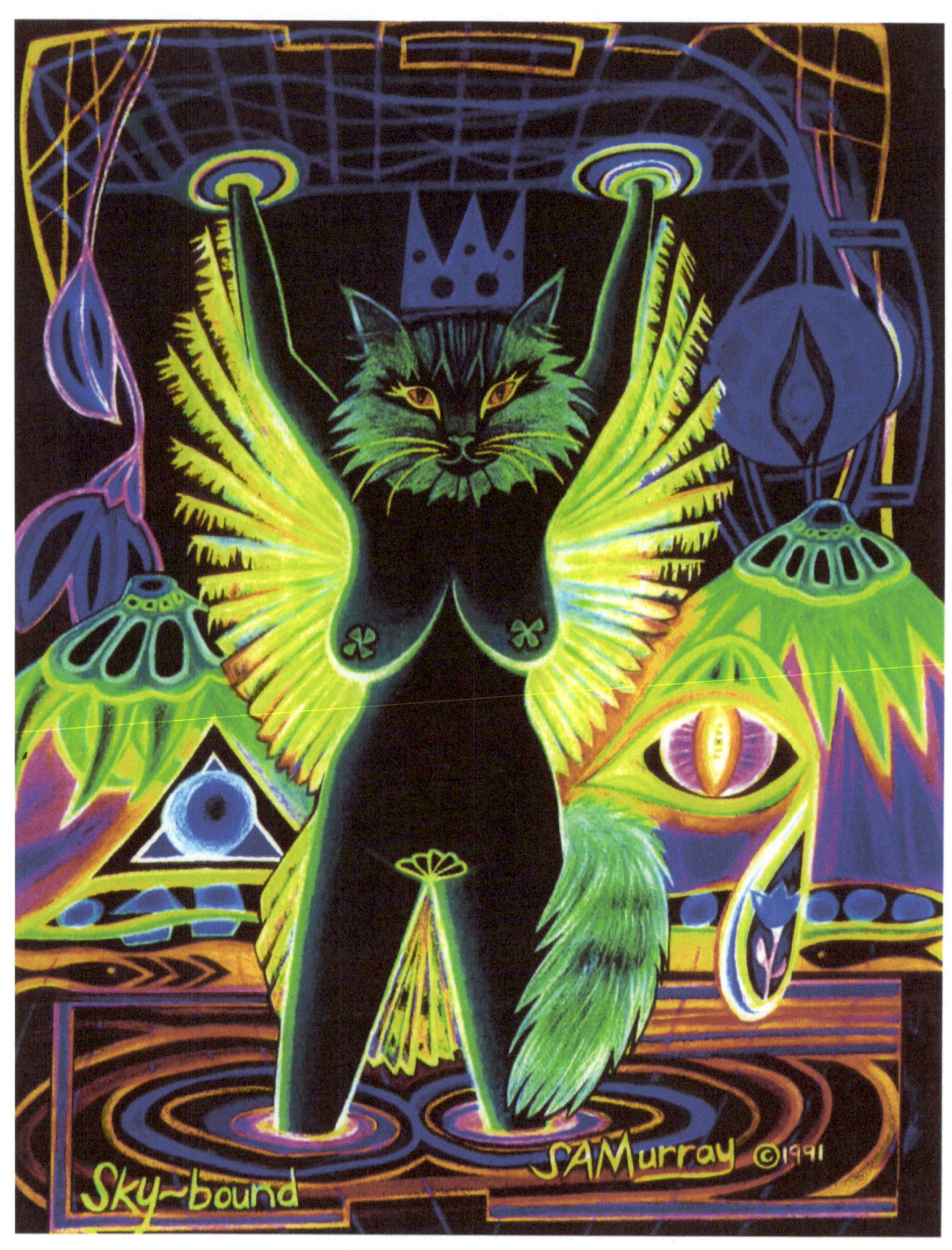

SKYbound

crazy world

why   sometimes
does this   crazy world
make sense when none exists

chaos lines up
circling   in a random order

why   sometimes
does insanity   come clear
and mean   more than sanity
ever could

and while   Jupiter
takes a cosmic beating
and man   stays trapped
in a half-full   moon

I feel the smallest
the most   invisible
amongst it all

when will   my world
make sense again?

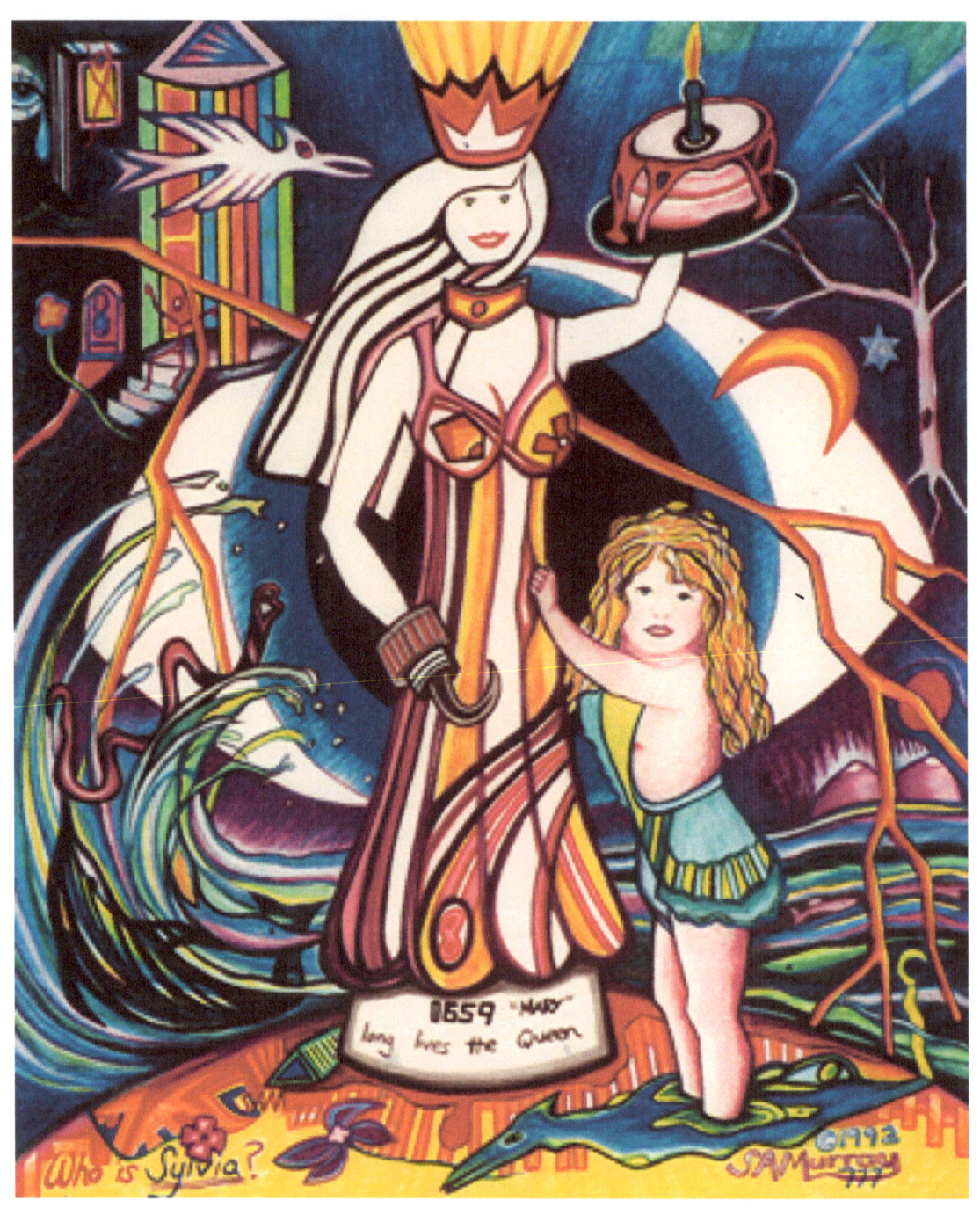

Who is Sylvia?

at 17

I knew too much
too much to contain

it spilled out
the eyeholes
became art
poetry
dance
beauty
too much to contain

but they tried
to box me
and I spilled out
imploded
exploded
escaped
rebuilt

and lived again

chained again and again
I contained myself
imploded
ceased to breathe
tread carefully
stifled exuberance
too much too much

I would rather
hold my breath
contain half
of too much
**then be locked in
forever**

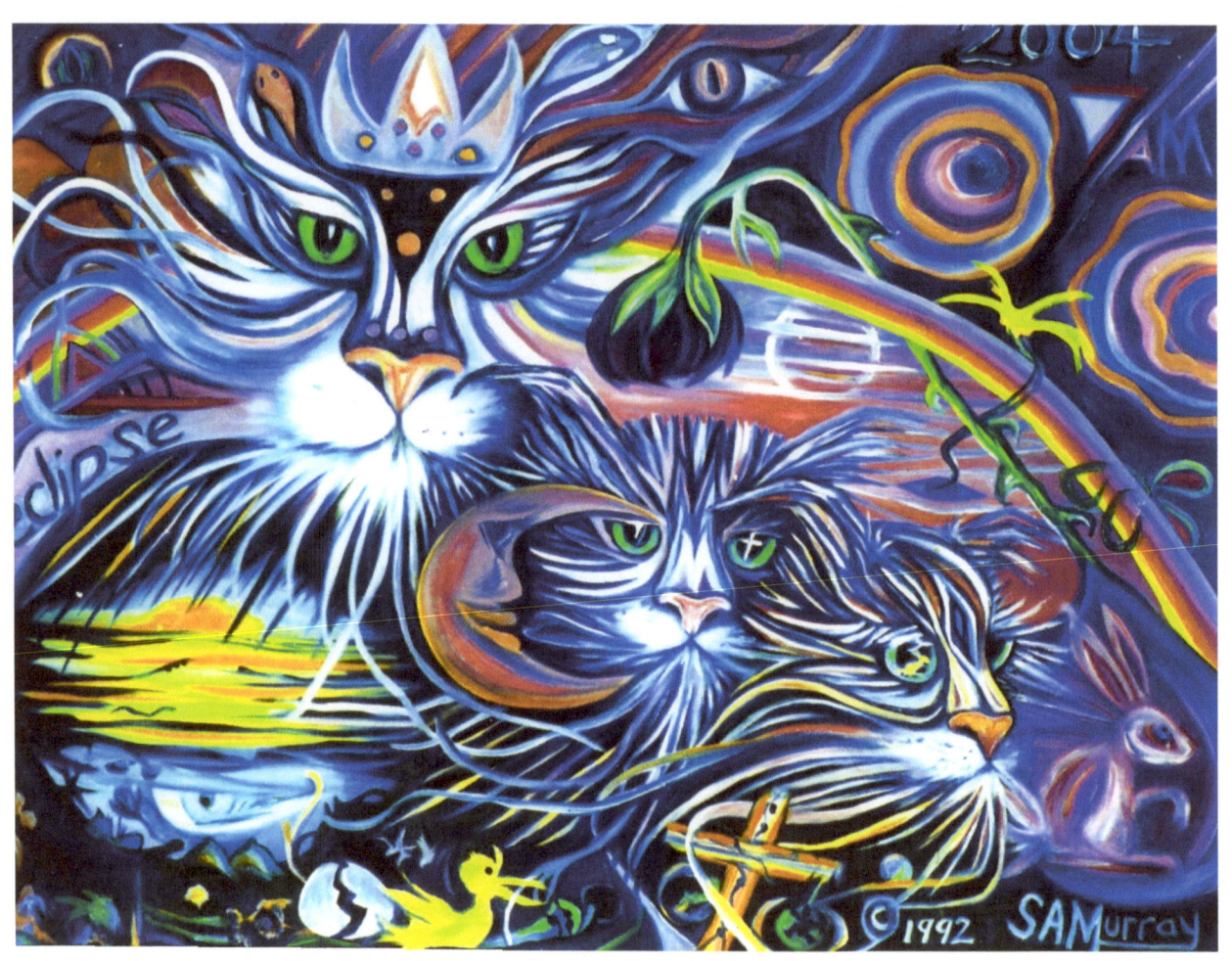

Cosmic Cats

Up-side   Down

I have been   Up-side Down
buried under   piles of fur
shed by ancient Cats

when   the Sun rises
I crawl in   under
hide   sleep
til meows and darkness
tap me   on the butt
saying   wake up! wake up!
We are the Meowers
of modern times
the Guardians   of your Mind
and we demand   your attention!

the Moon-light   keeps me company
the Meows   grate on me
reminding   "I am Alive!"

the Back-wards Cycle
Strokes   my Mind
as the Future flows
thru my   Finger tips
Smacking loudly   against a History
of Queens   Insane   be-headed
with no King   to guard the Castle

So it is   "I am"
Around around
and always   Up-side Down!

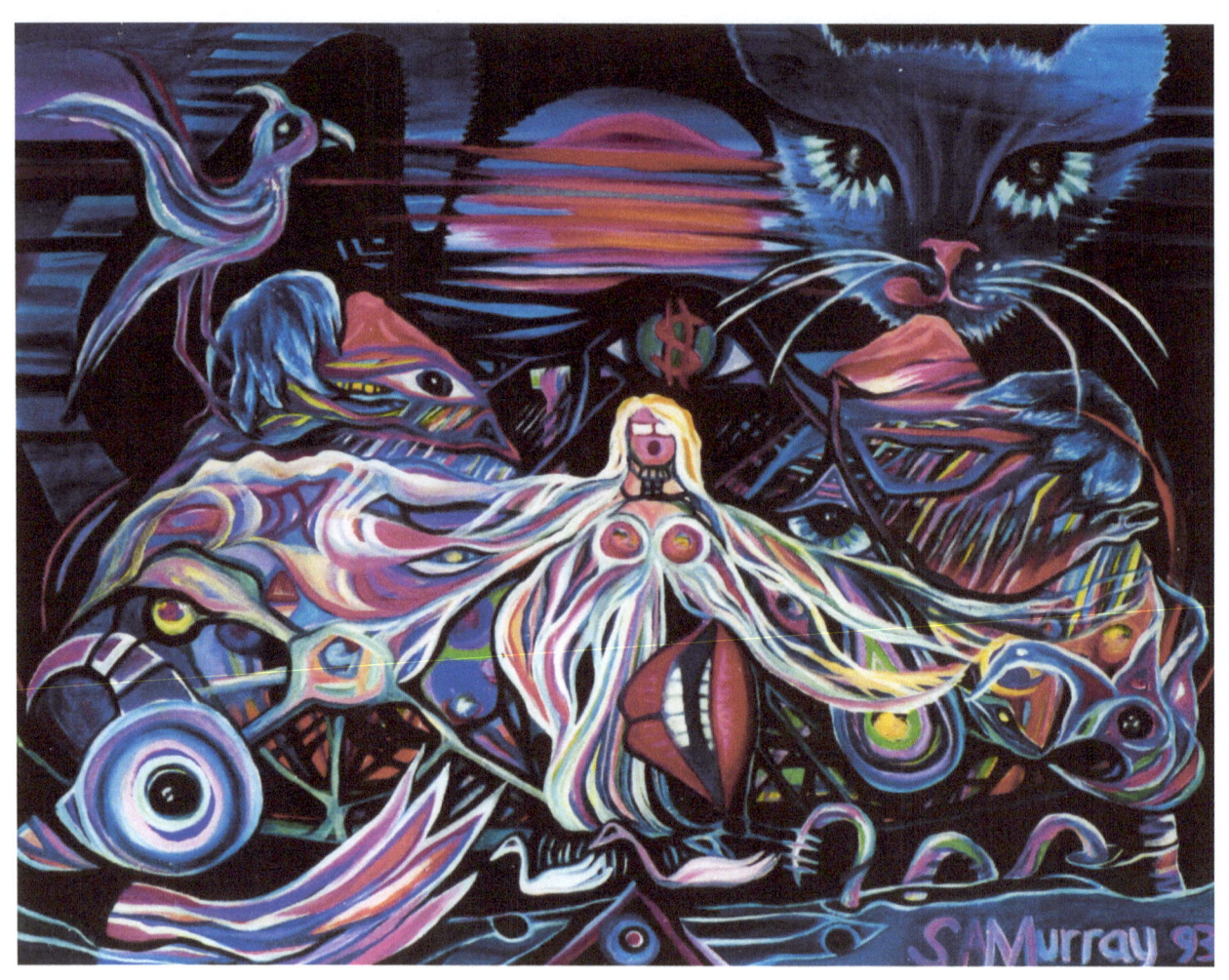

Lady Liberty

L A D Y   L I B E R T Y

I want to perch
atop the world
surrounded by people
who do not sense
my presence

to make the announcement
that would save Mankind
if anyone could hear
my velvet voice
falling softly
between the trees
in that Forest
where no one
felt the world E N D

I want my energy
to glow in the F I R E
that doesn't burn
and quench the thirst
of a humankind
that never knew the T R U T H

I want the T R U T H
to be Free and Wet
for all to partake of
and then I want
to become the S K Y

and on the last day
I want only to F L Y

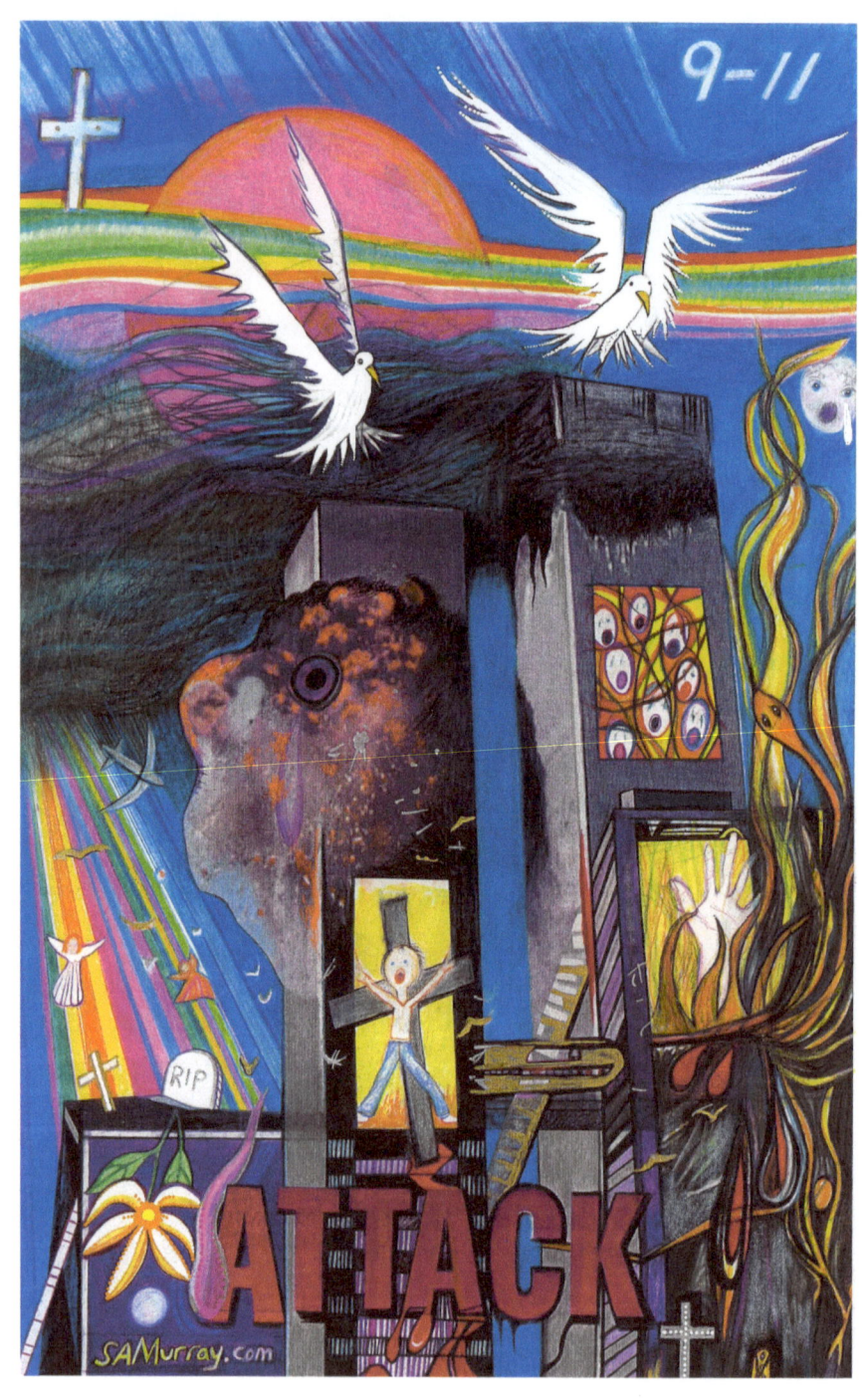

911 Attack

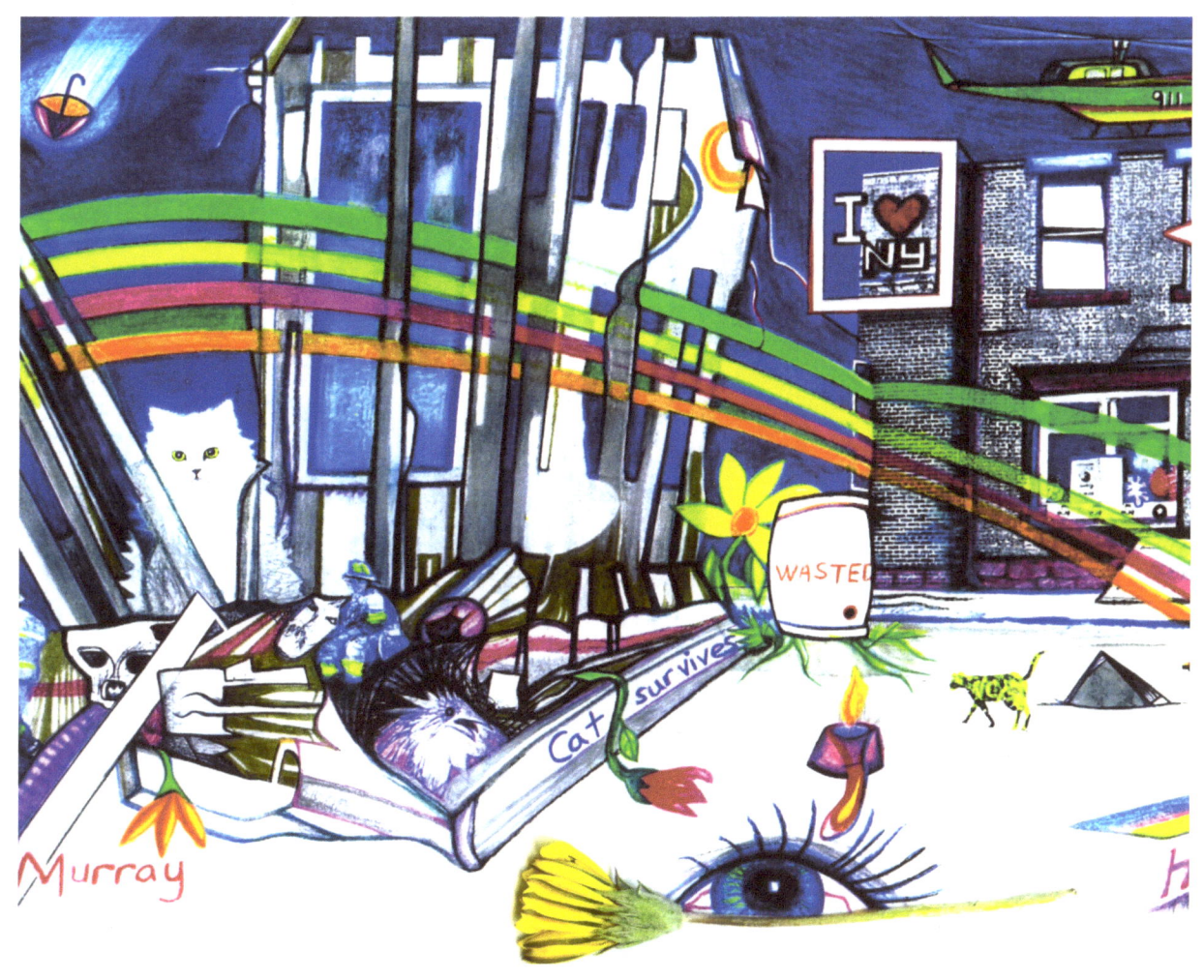

Hope Emerges

Blue-eyed Child

I am the untouched
sealed behind steel mirrors
that conceal mysteriously the Blue-eyed Child
who cried out so many times
only to find her soul slapped into a corner
her eyes become the mirror
reflect the beauty trap the pain
when left behind travel the Insane
No-one could ever find me
so now we are many
reflections deceive illusions are plenty
I reflect the summer day
I feel quickly every way
I am an enclosed reflection
bent by many sunlights

Stone-child

I am the stone-child
shedding invisible tears
insides made of glass
broken in many pieces
I am clay
to the ocean's touch
so run in fear
of the water's edge
the salt seeks
out my pain
the feelings intense
I go Insane
I stand in the sand briefly
to become the child
I melt into the Ocean
crying out
feeling the pain
to come unglued
to feel the tears
the Ocean washes me away
left on the beach
one child at play

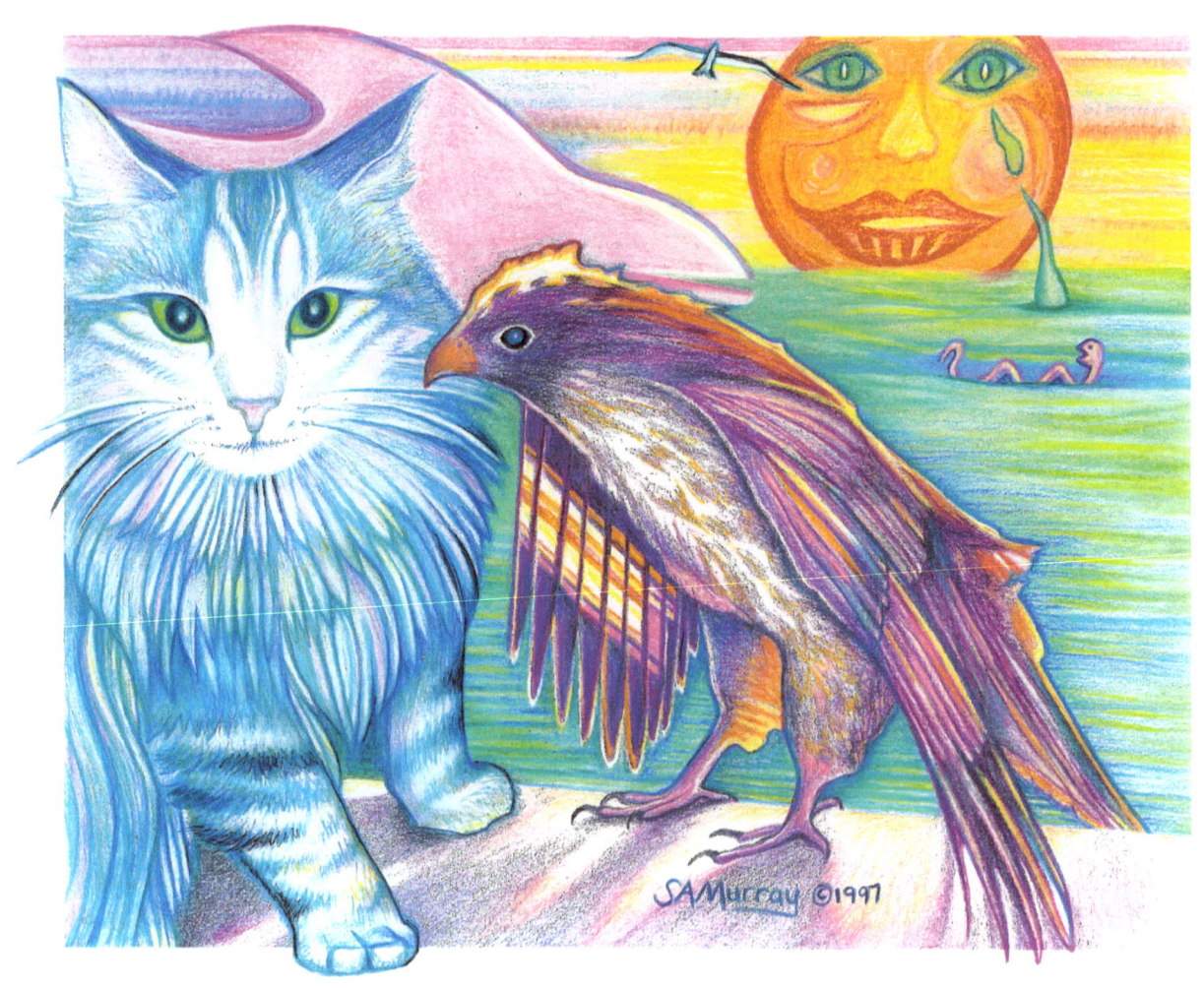

Soulmates

the world kaleido-scopes

and I shift comfortable
with the sliding
I see the shadows moving
knowing they aren't in our world
glancing around the corners
no one should see
feeling not alone
knowing the Truth
has layers not explained
walking in a Reality not real
knowing I am here for this
somehow the Message
multi-dimentional
comes thru my fingers
and will be Released

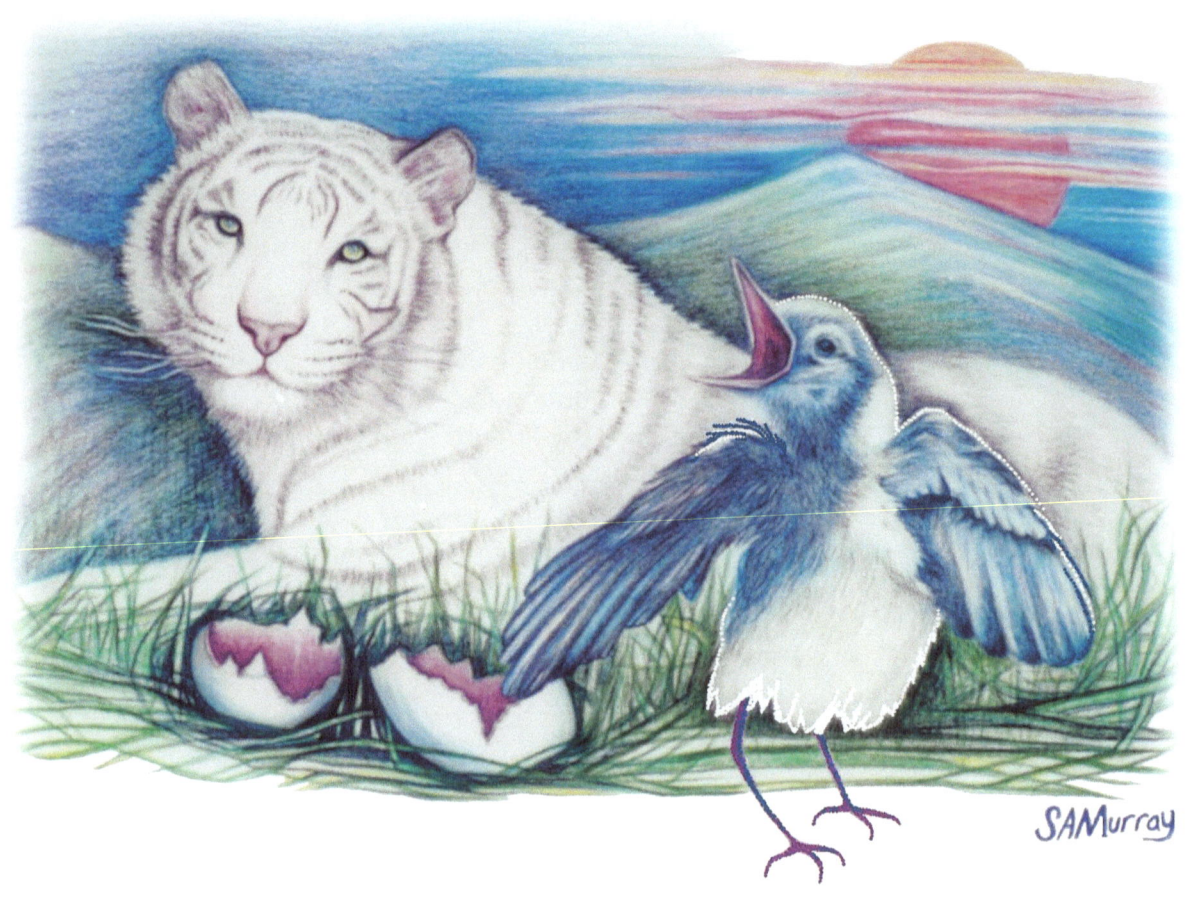

Harmony

Have you ever...

Have you ever
heard the voices
of the people in the elevator
moments before it stopped

empty on your floor

or seen the figure
of a person
not actually there

Do you know the presence
of the   lady
who lived in your space
who passed in quiet grace

listening to the voices
around   surround
wondering   what people do
to carry on

feeling the Peace of the Winged Ones
brush me   gently
wondering   of the lightness
in Heaven

sliding slipping into the Rainbow
one day to fly Free

Have you ever wondered Why
Have you ever just known

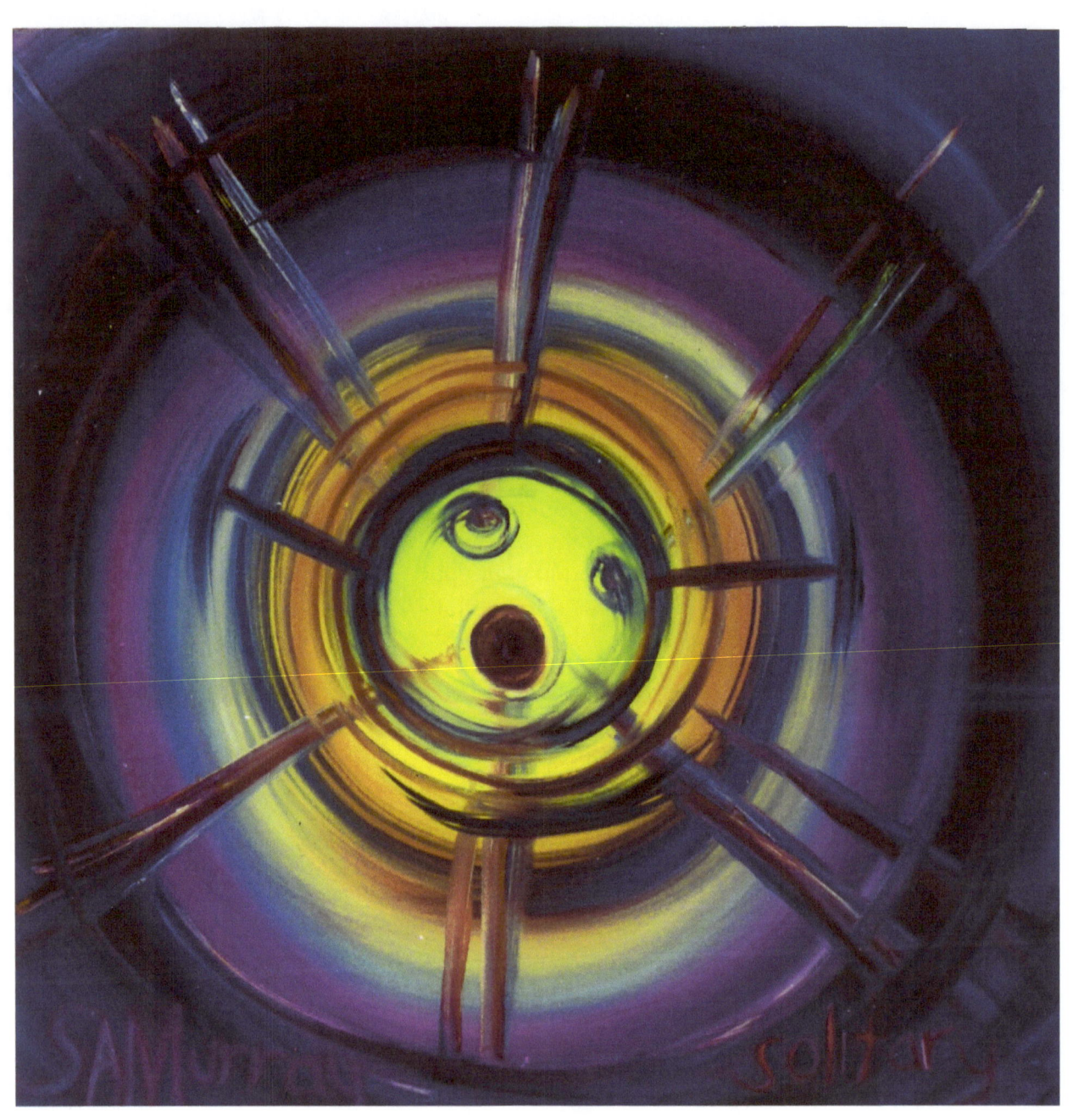

Scream

Runaway Train

there is that brief knowledge
that your mind has become a Runaway Train
then Awareness a quickening
into and beyond Insane
there is a merging into one raindrop
reading Eternity's Pain in a kitten's cry
the meow of the wild condensed by the city
wailing to be Free
and then there is You
You are the Runaway Train

the Gods have wings

yes the Heavens are above us
yes the Gods have wings
yes there is peace in the air
yes the birds Know
they know without thoughts
they travel Freely in random order
their lives make sense they fly Free
soar and dip play and smile
yes the Heavens are above us
and Peace can be found
harmony and wings
and on the last day
I only want to Fly

for V I N C E N T

only yesterday
I passed you
on your way to Rest
I have come A L I V E
my Soul E x p l o d e d
upon canvasses
for all to see

and you have finally died
and passed it safely
for me to carry on

yes I was there
with you and still
carry the P A I N
I have been there
I know I N S A N E

but I have come back
to set you F R E E
you can   go Home   now
to the Fields and the Sky

we are O N E
we passed in this L I F E
I will continue your Spirit
in this earthly body

together   one day
the daisies will dance
upon graves of A R T I S T S
who can n e v e r die

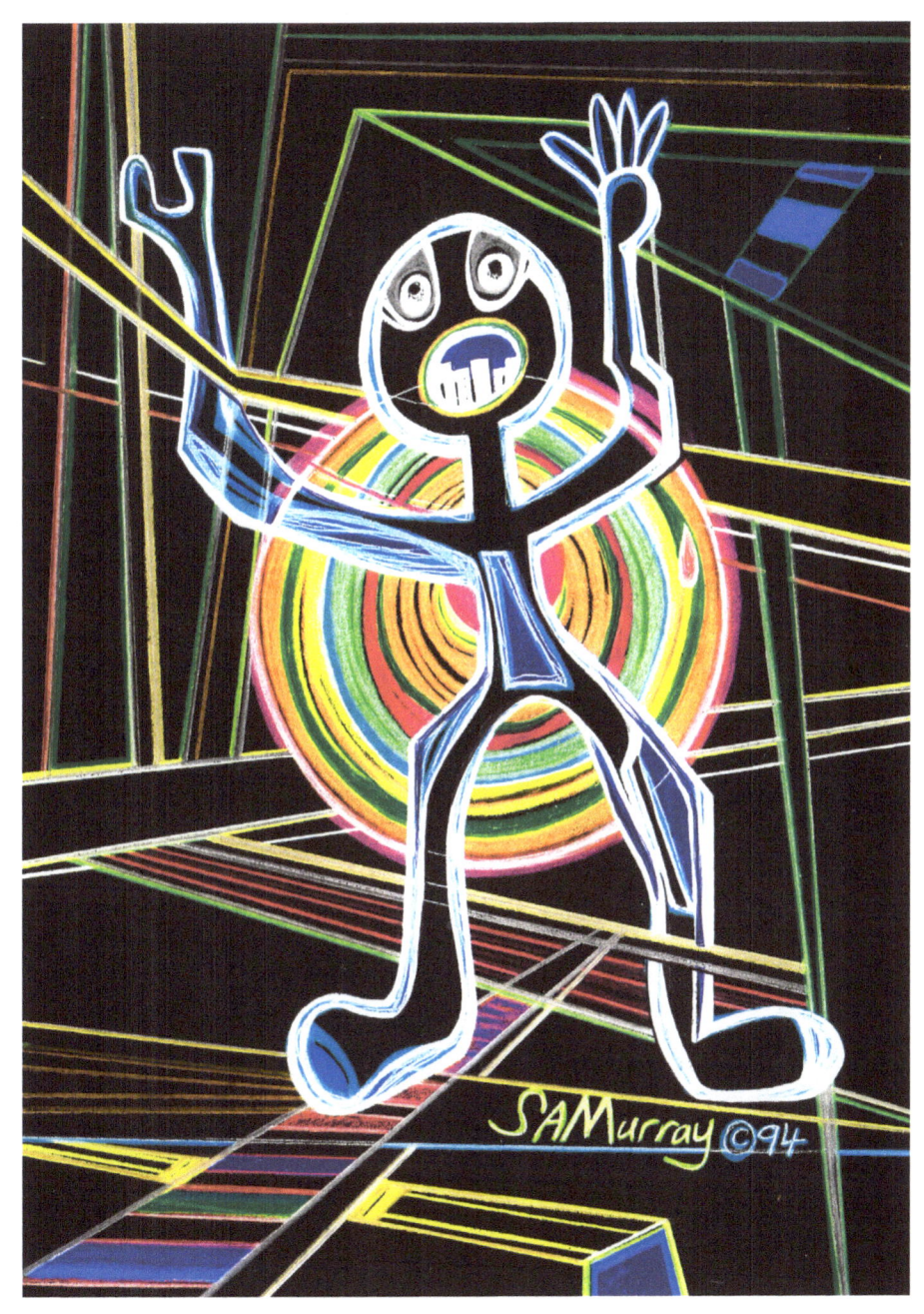

Mankind Screams

we ALL fade

some whimpering alone
behind closed doors
some screaming
losing our minds
forgetting who we are
some go quickly overnight
not a sound
part of a dream
some of us are here
for mysterious reasons
and leave messages
for our cats to read
closed paws
canvasses
become scratching posts
will we ever know why
and what
will become of us
after we are gone
- - - - - -
I want my ashes
scattered
among
the young
rebellious minds
fertile for the new
open for the old
re-seeded
strong trees
emerge

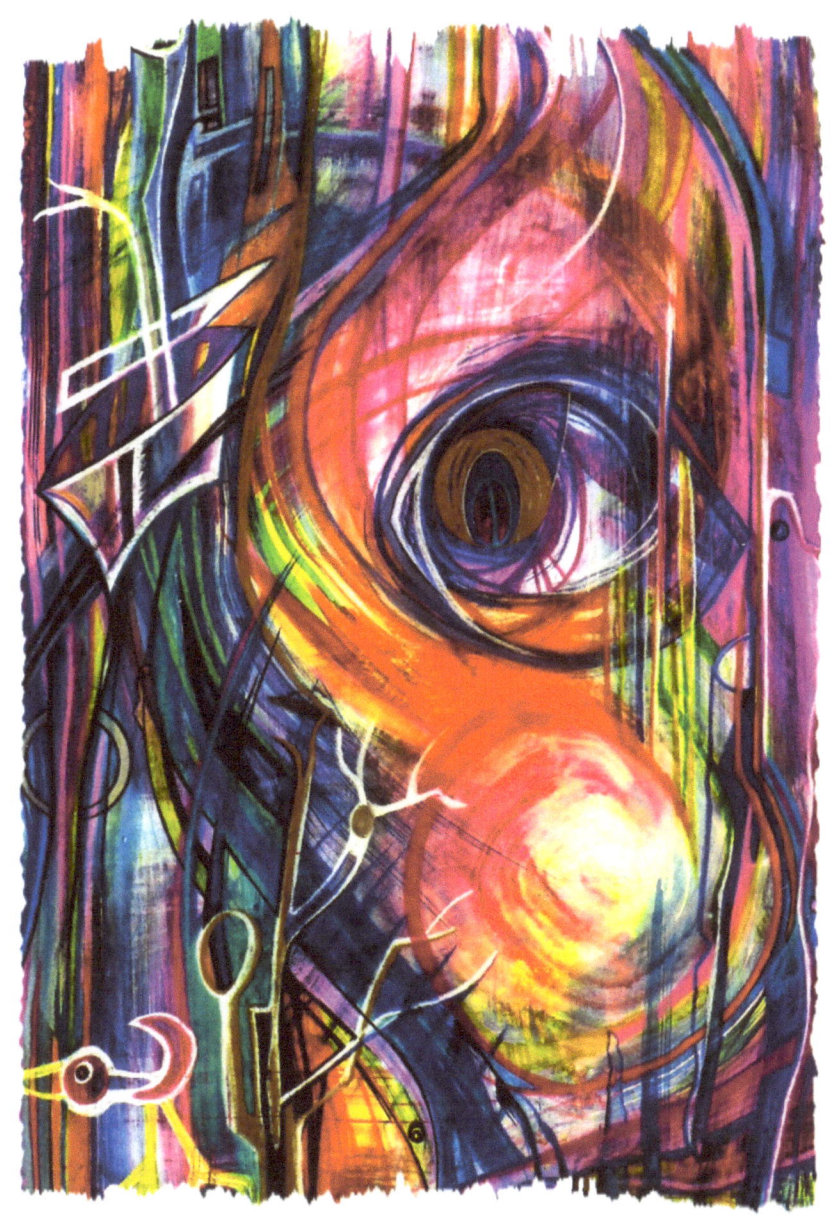

Meltdown

-D A M A G E-

the DAMAGE done leaks out my fingertips
landing upside down   on canvasses
            too strange   too clear

    It smacks you   in the face
        and as you turn   in horror
            to silently   slink away

    the DAMAGE grabs you   sits you down
            and screams WHY ME?
    It could be you   and you   and you

    I could lock you up   for years
            with   NO   EXIT
to see what accumulates   inside your brain
        to see if it leaks out anywhere
    to see if you live   to contain your PAIN
        on canvasses   for all to see

        Canvasses   that follow you
            home at night

    But you are   strangely SANE
        and you   can go home
            and sleep   in the dark

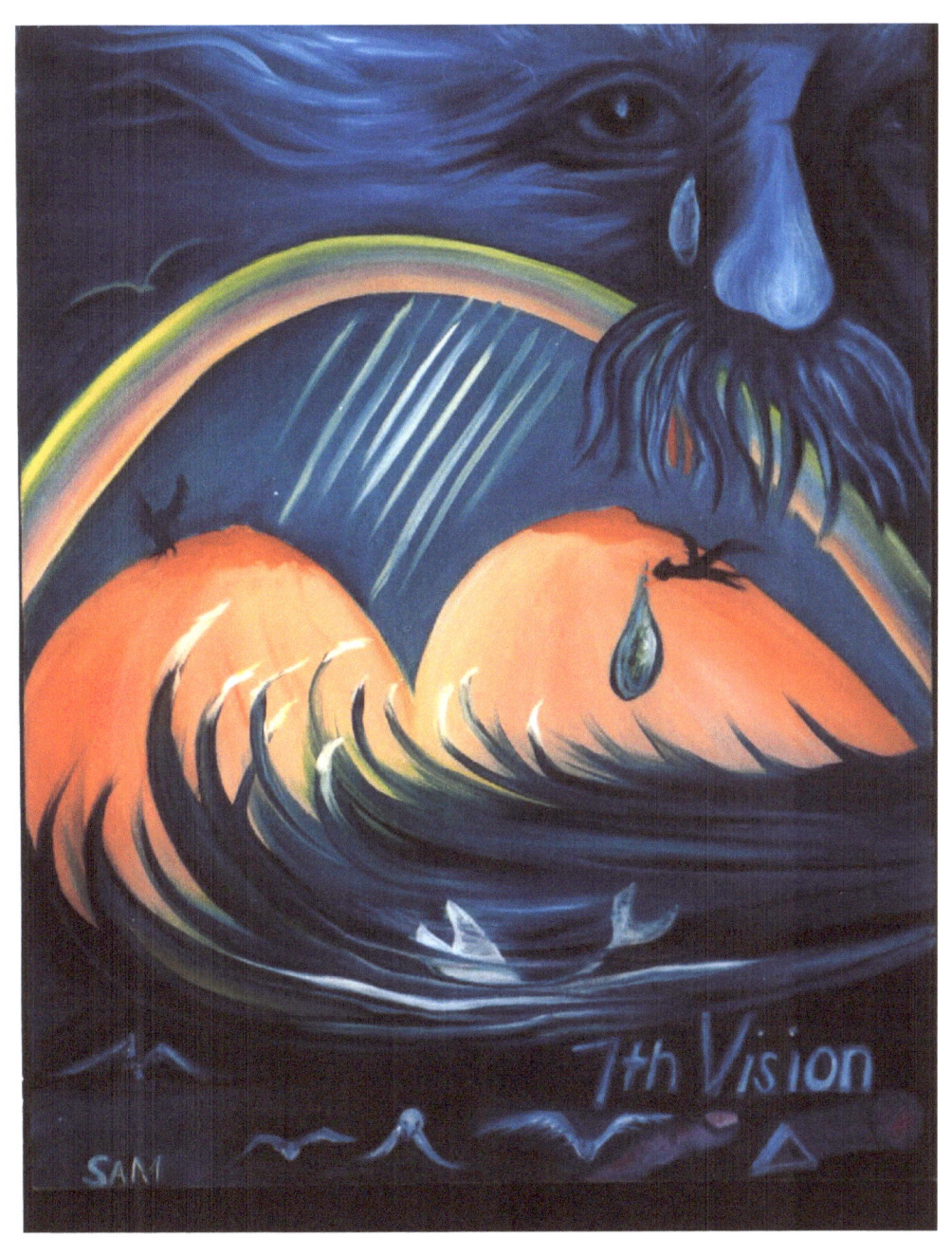

7th Vision

T U R N I N G   a corner

I feel   the bend-ing   softly
We are T U R N I N G a corner
We are all   an-other
of   our-selves
and see things a new

We can   B E G I N   again

the   S U N shines intensely
through dark glasses
We glow   and know
We are Not   R E A L

We bend   a little
and roll   away
coming   back   to join
a New Body   ever ves cent
Our   S O U L S
will   carry us
thru   the Dark-ness

We   find   P E A C E
in the   after-glow
and start   a journey
of   Open ing

E M E R G I N G   grad u all y
from a box   so cold

hold   to the L I G H T
escaping   the box
standing   child-like

glowing   in the S U N

H U M A N I T Y open-ed   Eyes
knows the J O U R N E Y
has   just   b e g u n

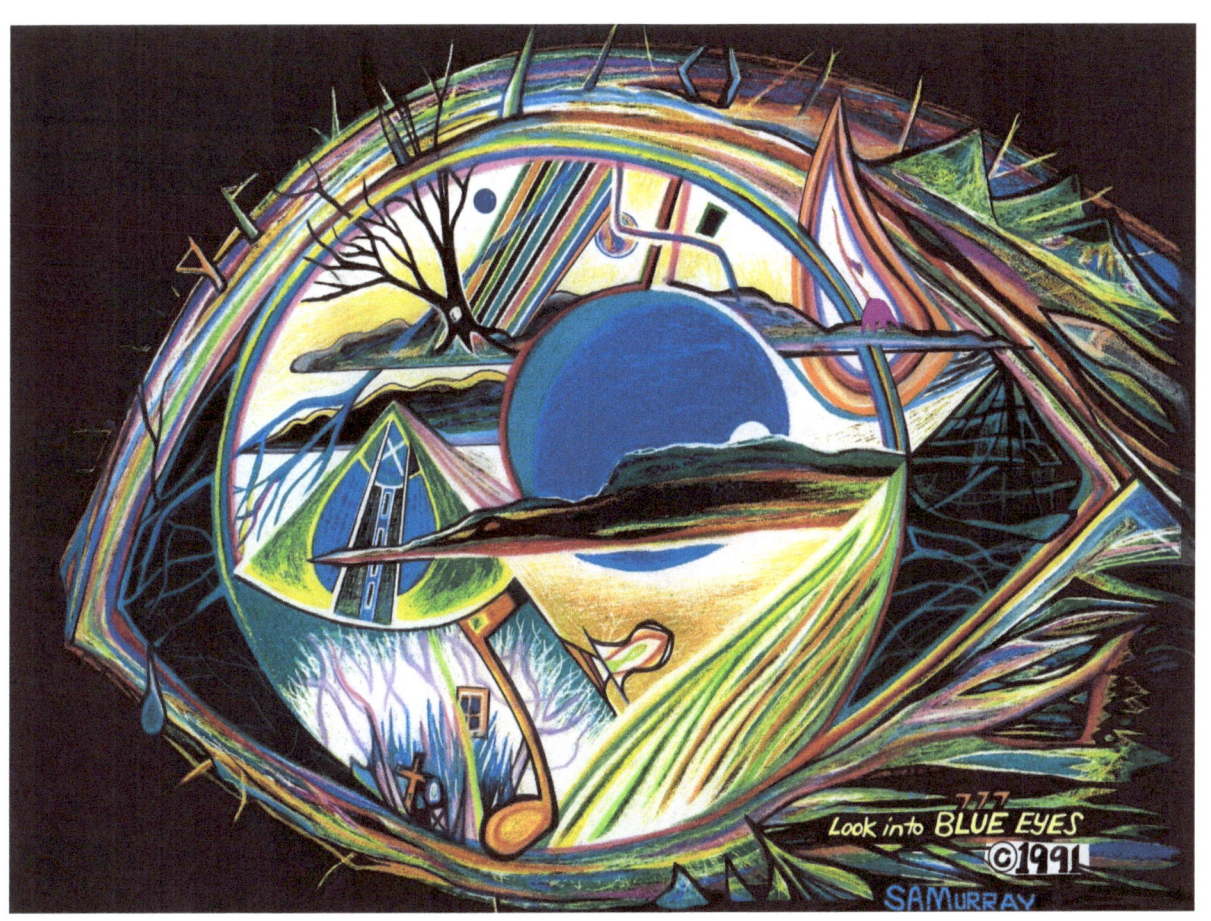

Blue Eyes

HOUSE

I live   in a house
of   o p e n windows
and shut   d o o r s

Birds   fly in and o u t
CATS s m i l e
and keep   h o u s e   all day

I am the   in side
and   out side
I have   the key
To the   only door

I F L Y   by
in and out
when S U N S H I N E
sings s a f e t y

by N I G H T
I join   both worlds
in a S O U L
left   long ago
over   the O C E A N

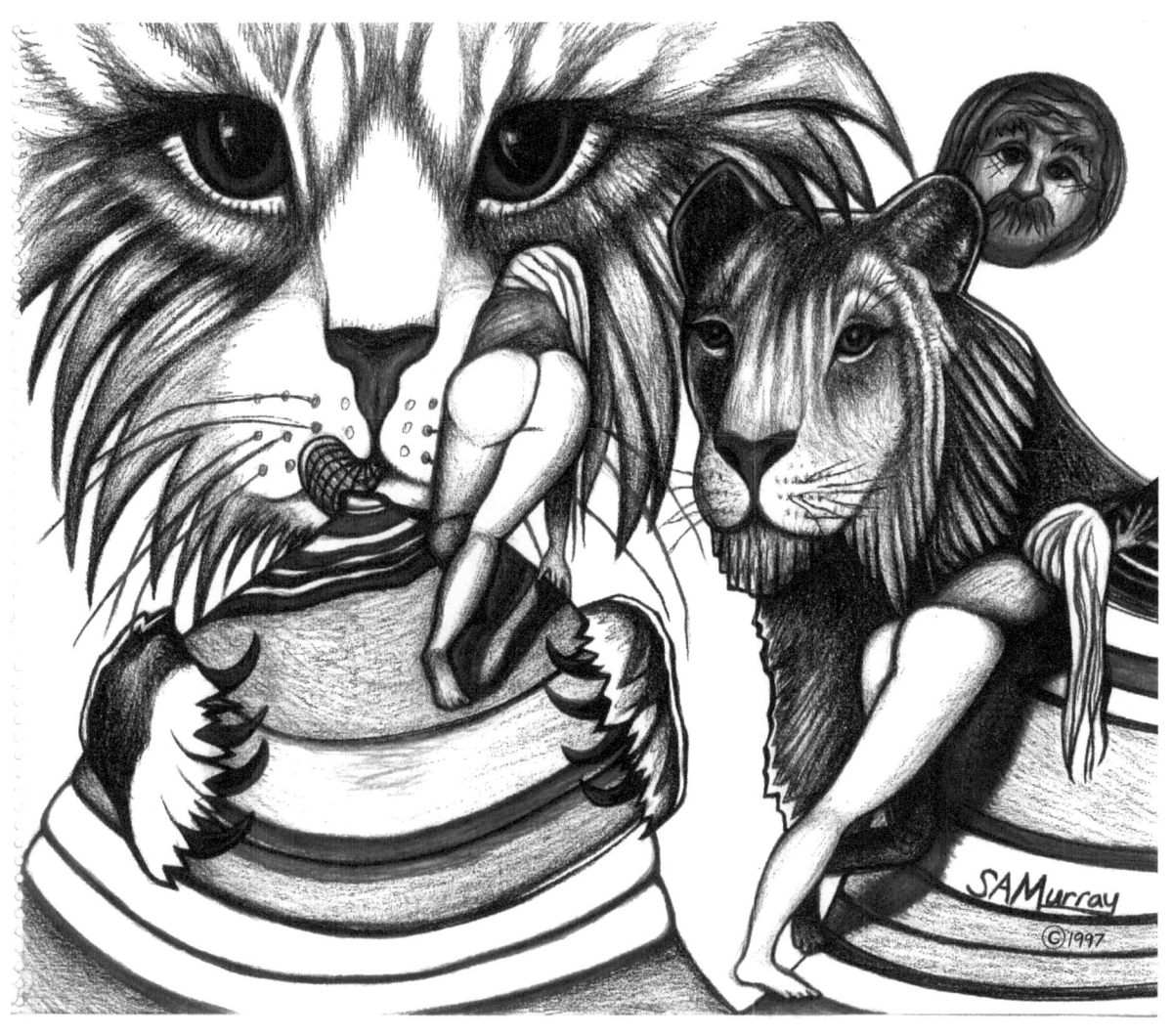

Nudes Climbing

I AM

Caught between   two Raindrops
on the way   to find the   Sun
slipping   sliding sideways
finding myself   a lightening bolt
unleashed

careful   careful   when I   strike
striking   not to blind   Mankind
but to enlighten   electrify
wake up   wake up
hitch-hiking cosmic riding
on a falcon's back

Searching for a   forest

in which to   find   myself
or perhaps   to   disappear
to rejoin the   tree of Life   that I am
silent   into Eternity
the Wisdom   quiet
until lightning   strikes

I am at the start   eons ago
I am the Violet   in the Rainbow
painted in my first   painting

I am the blueness in my eyes
I am the Rainbow   upside down
circling the full   Moon
I AM

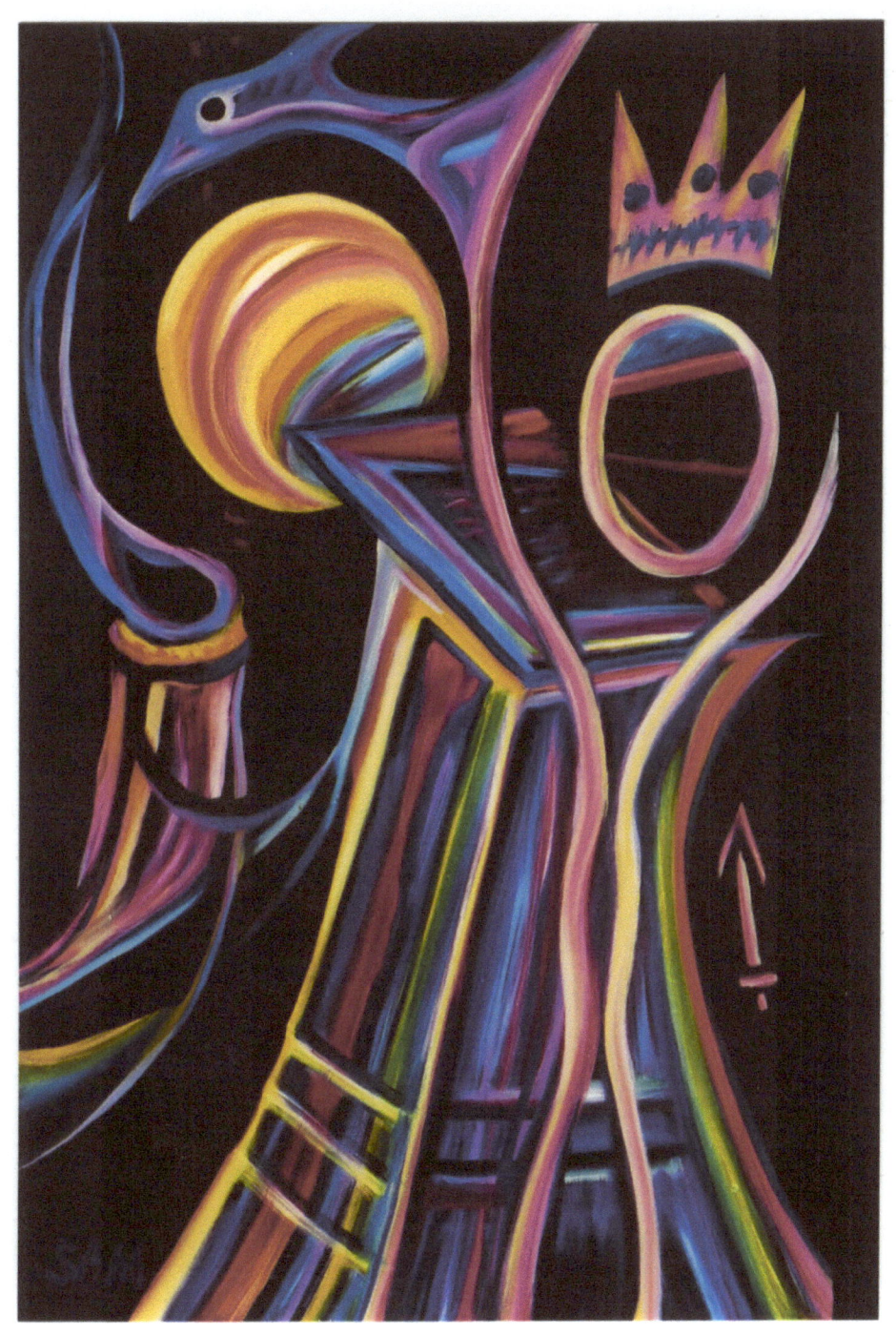

Mankind

r e s t l e s s

I am too r e s t l e s s
to sit still

feel tiny explosions
as I step
and know I have
to move quickly
as the world is shifting

I must not be caught
over the edge of the cliff
that will appear
when I relax too soon

no one is there
to calm me
and no one knows why

I am a spark
restless on the ocean
never quite cooled
by the water
I am suspended above

42

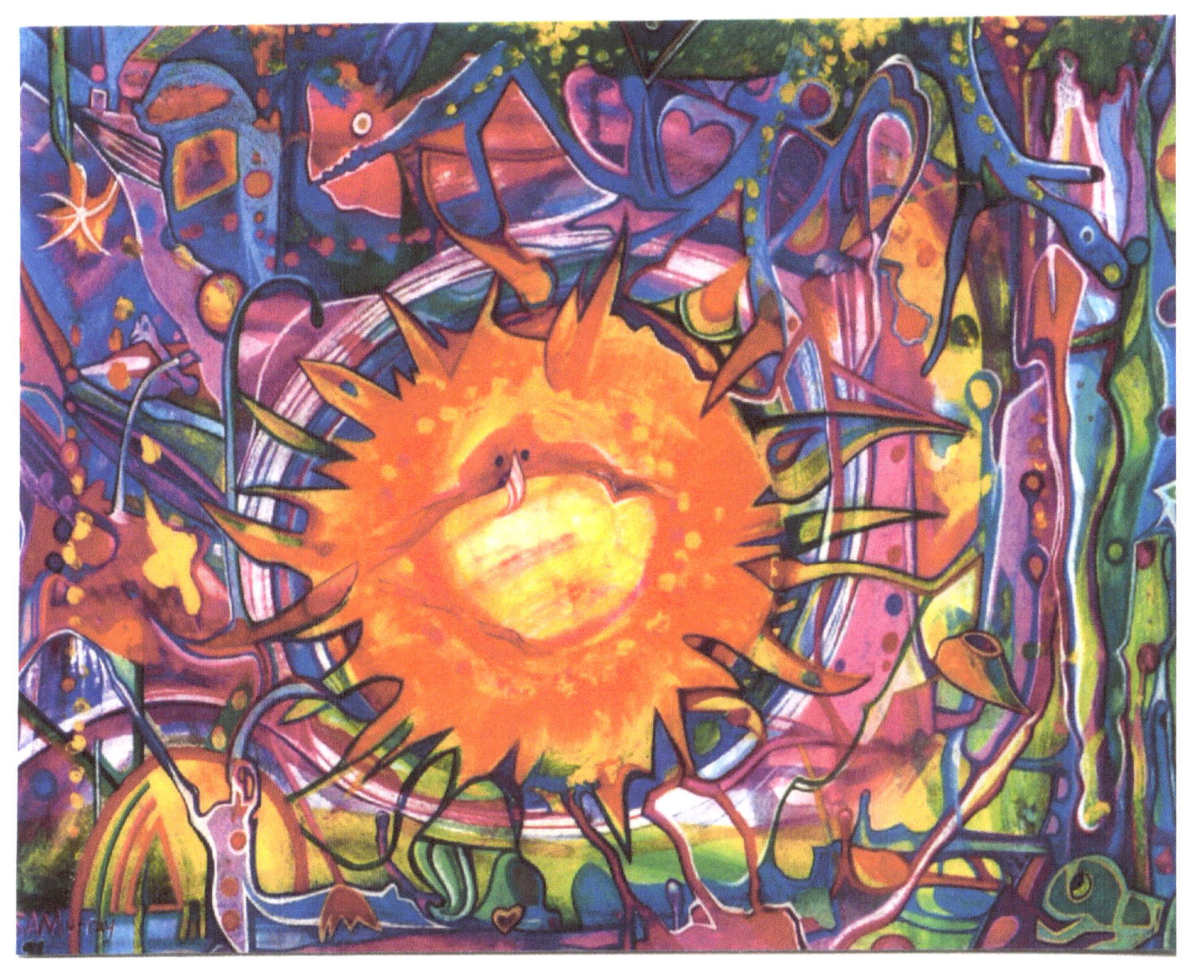

Sunburst

the M A N I C

chasing   stars
in far away   galaxies
circled   the M O O N
obsessively   driven
to her   cosmic   goal

only to   lose direction
as the   S U N S E T
blinded her

thumped   suddenly   in to
the solid   brown   E A R T H

found   her W I N G S   gone
be came   an   earth worm

grounded   felt the P A I N
of a suffering   Humanity
shouting   O U T
between   the Trees

E M E R G E D   a   Daffodil

one day she   will
F L Y again

Shattered in LA

LA is tapping
rapping ever louder
on my brain
LA won't allow space
for free flowing ideas
LA is smashing my head
into little pieces
I am frantic
trying to retrieve them
and at the next Red Light
I may give up
clutching onto strangers
who move away
I can only close my eyes
and pray

I am writing

I am writing on glass windows
gazing upward at blue skies
I am writing on the mirror
in invisible ink
staring at blue eyes
I am breaking thru
the barriers
one at a time
smashing into Eternity
I am Alone
and reaching out
become the mirror
falling into blue skies
I reflect the Universe
I am lost
behind glass doors
I will be the Sky

P E R F E C T   C H I L D

When I die
I will be four
once more

I will hold out my hand
beyond silver chains
and I will find my Father
this time

He will not hide behind an iron mask
and tell me I am not perfect
for I will always be
the Perfect Child

No longer will my tears
fall upon deafened ears
No longer will I be stopped
from running to the Ocean

I will open my eyes
to all once denied
I will mount my eagle
and encounter FREEDOM

I will entwine with elusive clouds
becoming the Rainbow of Hope
God promised eons ago
and it will be
Now and Forever

Blackness will
become golden sunlight
and I will find ETERNITY
holding my Father's hand
sliding down a Moonbeam

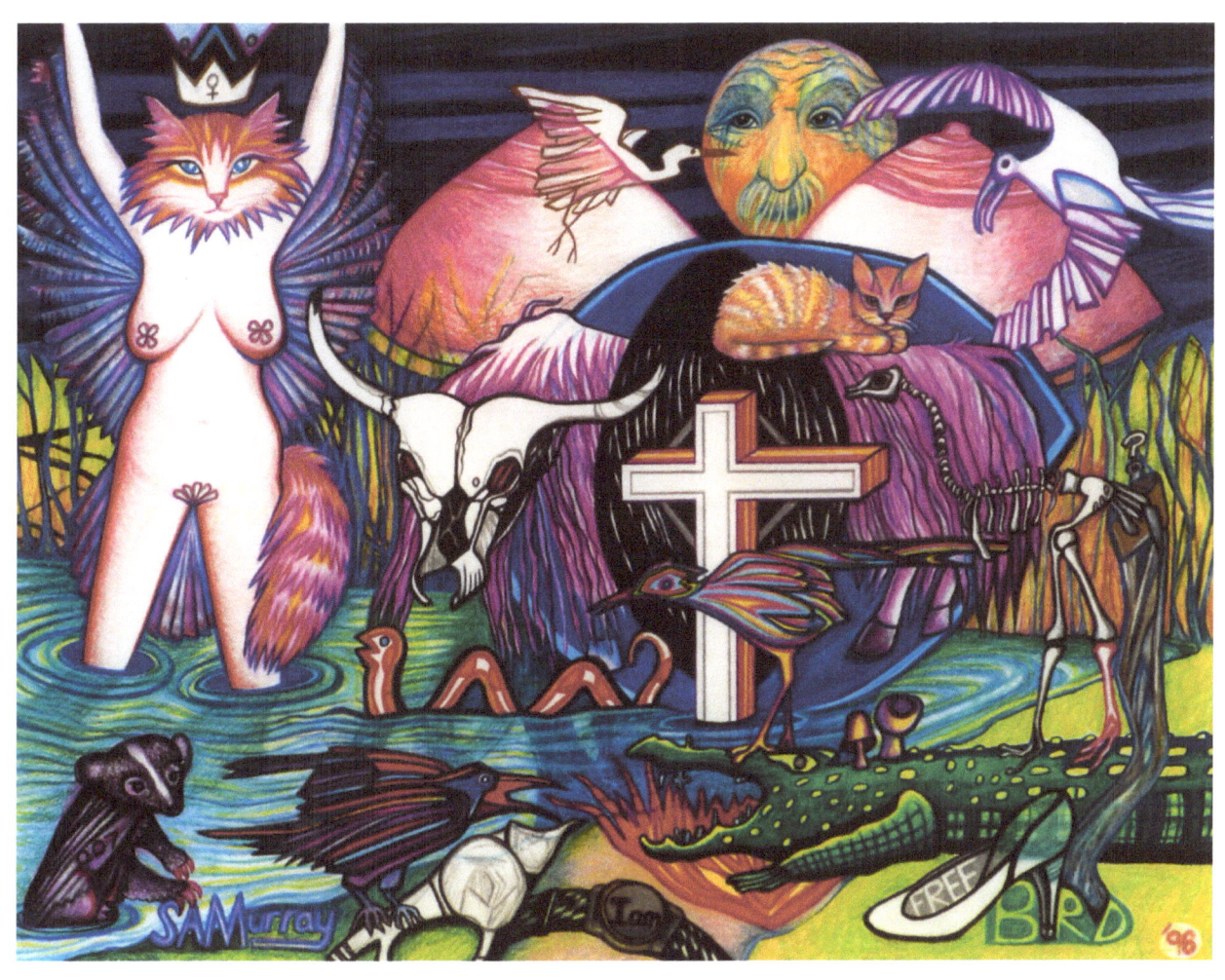

Free Bird

the RAINBOW

some times I wonder
who is holding ME
then realize
no one ever has
I have swung ALONE
high and low
some times se cure
some times coming a p a r t
always moving a head

through some times some times
finding the End of a dark tunnel
be fore glimpsing the RAINBOW

it is the RAINBOW that holds me
some times slip ping thru
stuck on the Pink or the Blue

and with RAINBOW vision
I see the white Light
and feel the purple PAIN
See with the Clarity
of the Wise One
some times feel the quest ions
of the INSANE

the RAINBOW
may be invisible to some
but the double circles
wrapped around the Moon
are always mine to keep

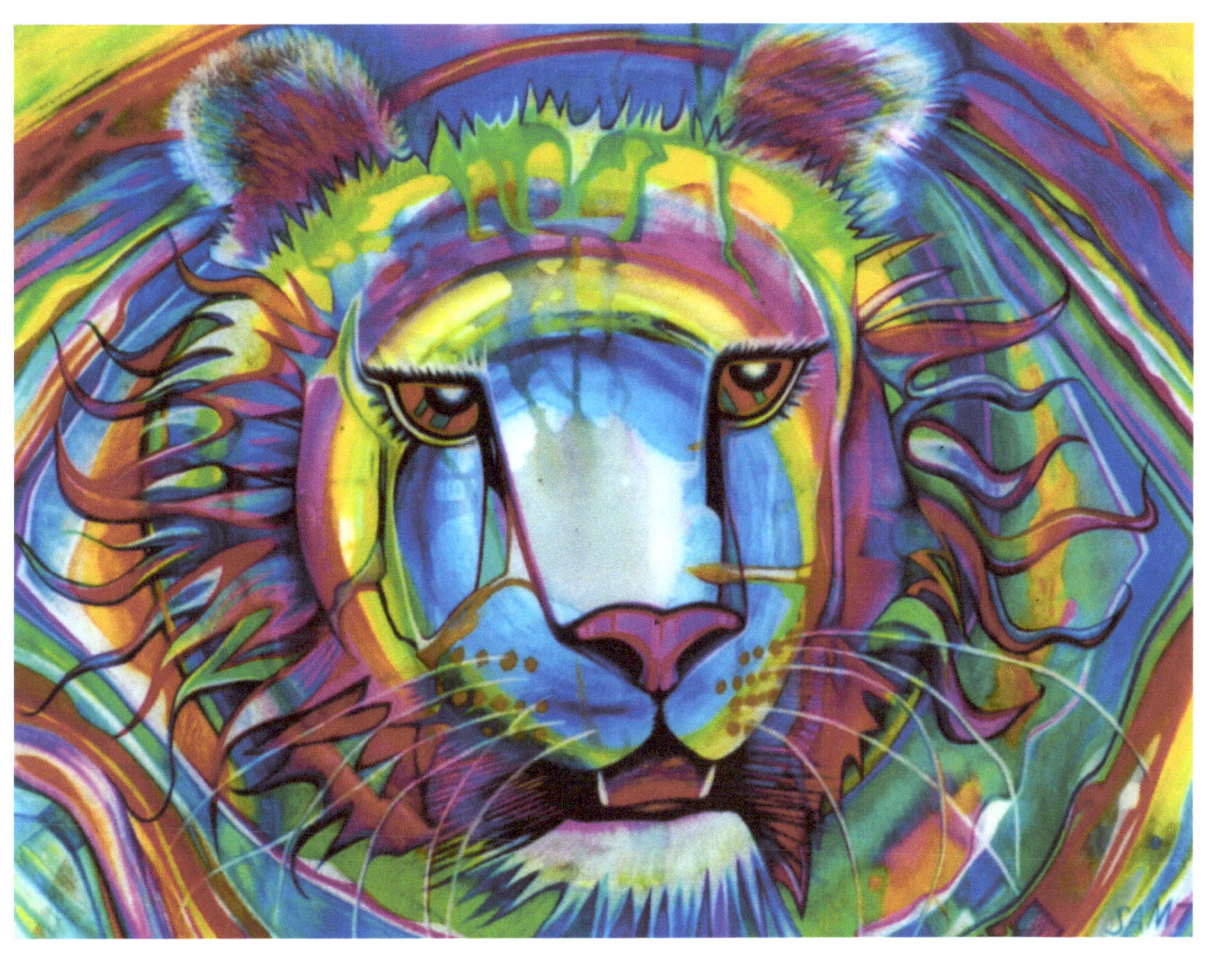

Rainbow Tiger

silence

in the silence
I find myself
an echo
bouncing off
every tree
in the universal forest

finding myself
again
the last leaf
and every leaf

the collector
of a silence
that holds peace
deep within
overwhelming chaos
that makes up life

in the silence
all of me
comes back
and I find
my essence

the collector of eternity
still
always there
centered

I find peace

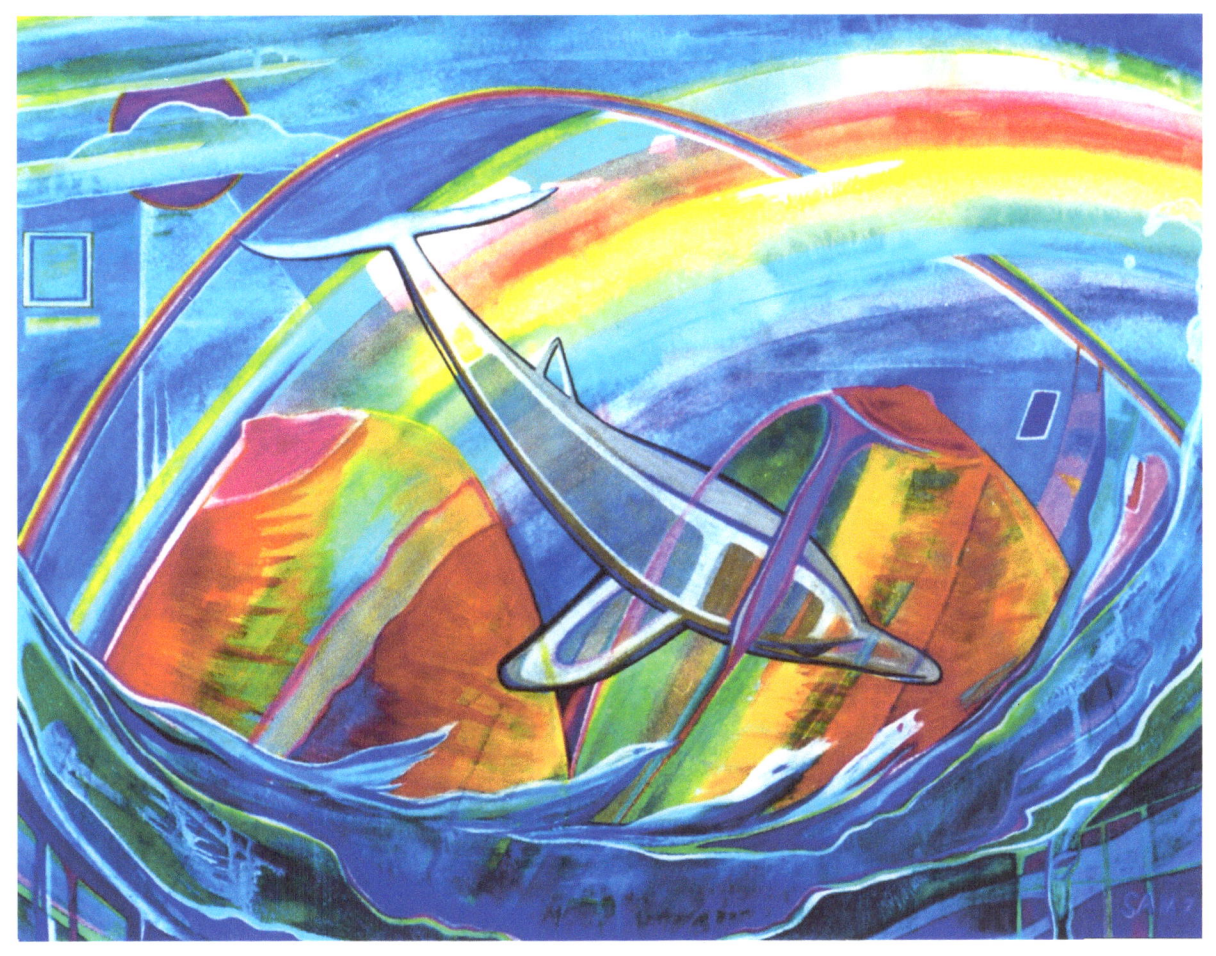

Rainbow VISION

P I N K

I feel W O U N D E D today

walked on   run over

wonder how I   lived
through the Twisted Mind
controlling me
Knowing   he makes NO sense
I still FEEL the   P A I N

and the (little) girl
curls up in a ball

Daddy please
don't kill me AGAIN
I am D E A D
I am D E A D   already

and she rocks her self
in a very different world
a PINK FEELING world
covering her self
in a P I N K blanket
a Shield to keep
the   Father Monster
O U T out (out)

he tells me   over and over
"You are a waste of time."

still he P O K E S at her
the P I N K does not
prevent the P A I N

no matter how far she retreats
the P I N K can not save (her)

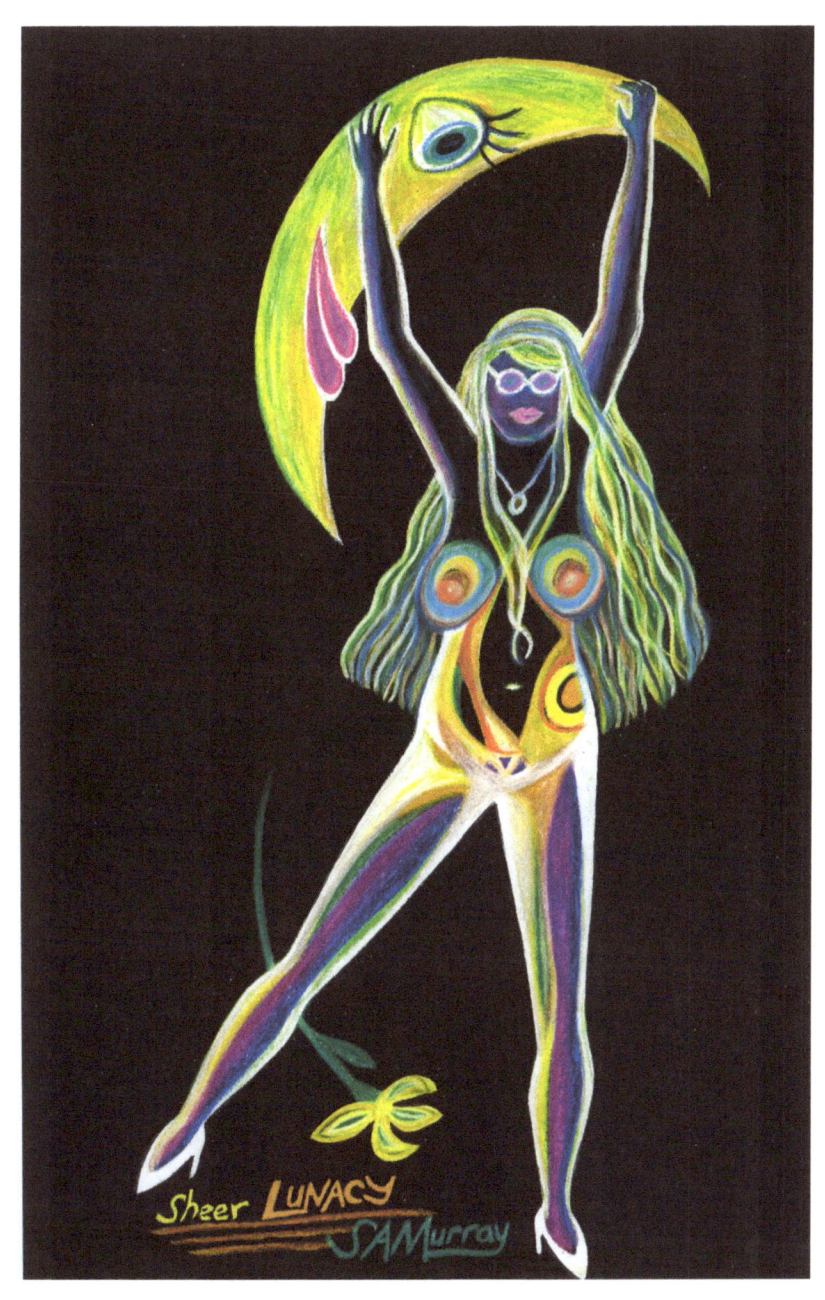

Sheer Lunacy

I hold my Breath

I hold my Breath
when the World   SQUEEZES
a little   tighter

I hold my breath   for days
and Hope I won't   E X P L O D E
as the M A D N E S S around me
tries   tries   over and over
to stop   my progress
to quell   my little Life

I breathe   ONLY when I feel
the air E X P A N D   again
I grapple   for a hold

I vow NOT   to let Go

calouses   on my hands   betray me
as I grip   tightly   the wheel
and avoid   over and over
the flash   of D E A T H

walking tip-toeing thru mine fields
I am   so care fully   still A L I V E
as the WORLD pauses   to exhale
and blue E Y E S open
to the WORLD   once again

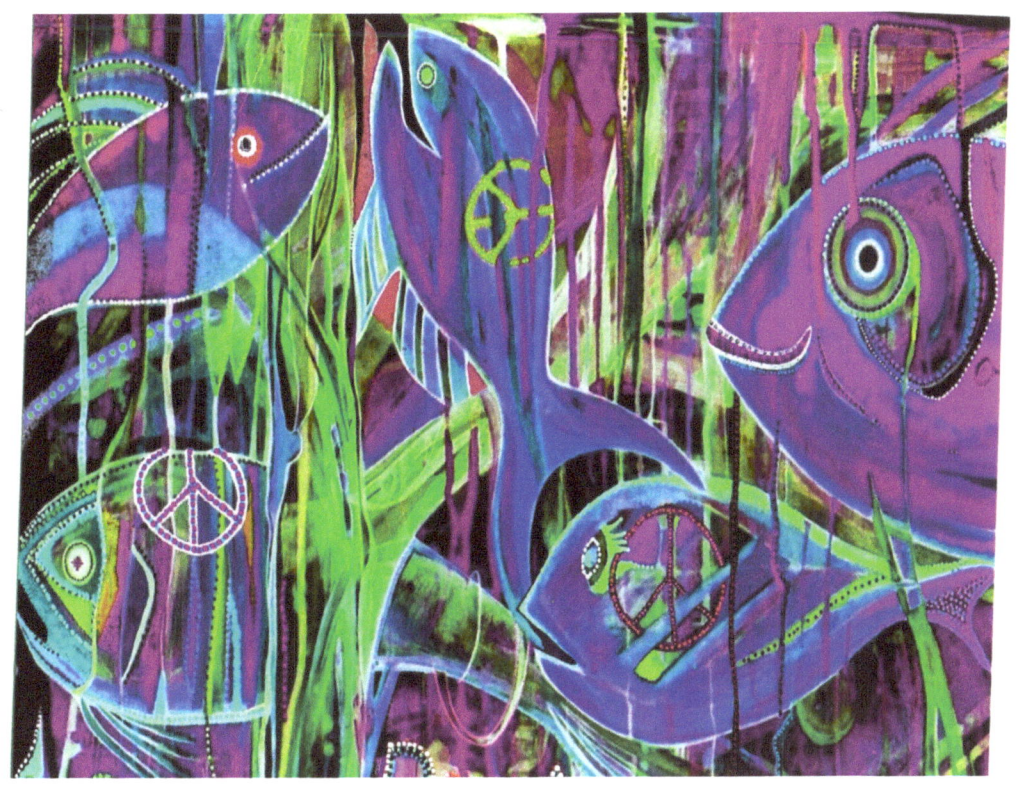

Psychedelic Fish

To My Peers: Focus on Hope

Why don't those of us advocating to stop the stigma around mental illness try focusing on more positive articles or stories and on the fact that many people who take their meds and work with their psychiatrist are stable, productive, and happy?

Now I am seeing more scary things on TV about mental illness and I am afraid it will snowball. There was such a horrible suicide attempt on a popular TV show that I could not even watch it. Let's not let things get out of control!

Also, the judicial system is not treating the people with mental illness fairly. A 13-year-old boy was put in jail for 25 years when he obviously needs treatment. What a mess...

I'm not saying don't talk about all aspects of mental illness. I do talk about some terrible things I've experienced, but I tend to **Focus on Hope**...

But I don't see many folks talking about becoming stable and the hope of having a productive life. I just want the public to see some positive people too. I volunteer with many other folks with mental illness and we all get along.

Also—maybe this is my personal opinion—I don't think it is helpful to watch suicides (on TV or by detailed description) as it might cause others to copy that behavior. At the Clubhouse where I volunteer we have lost some much loved people to suicide. That is enough info. Most do not want to know how it was done. Those kinds of things get "stuck in my head" and the grief is much more painful. I just want to remember the person alive.

Anyway, we have all had different experiences and I am glad we are sharing them. One thing that really helps me is to go to Poetry Readings, tell my story, and create art.

-SA Murray

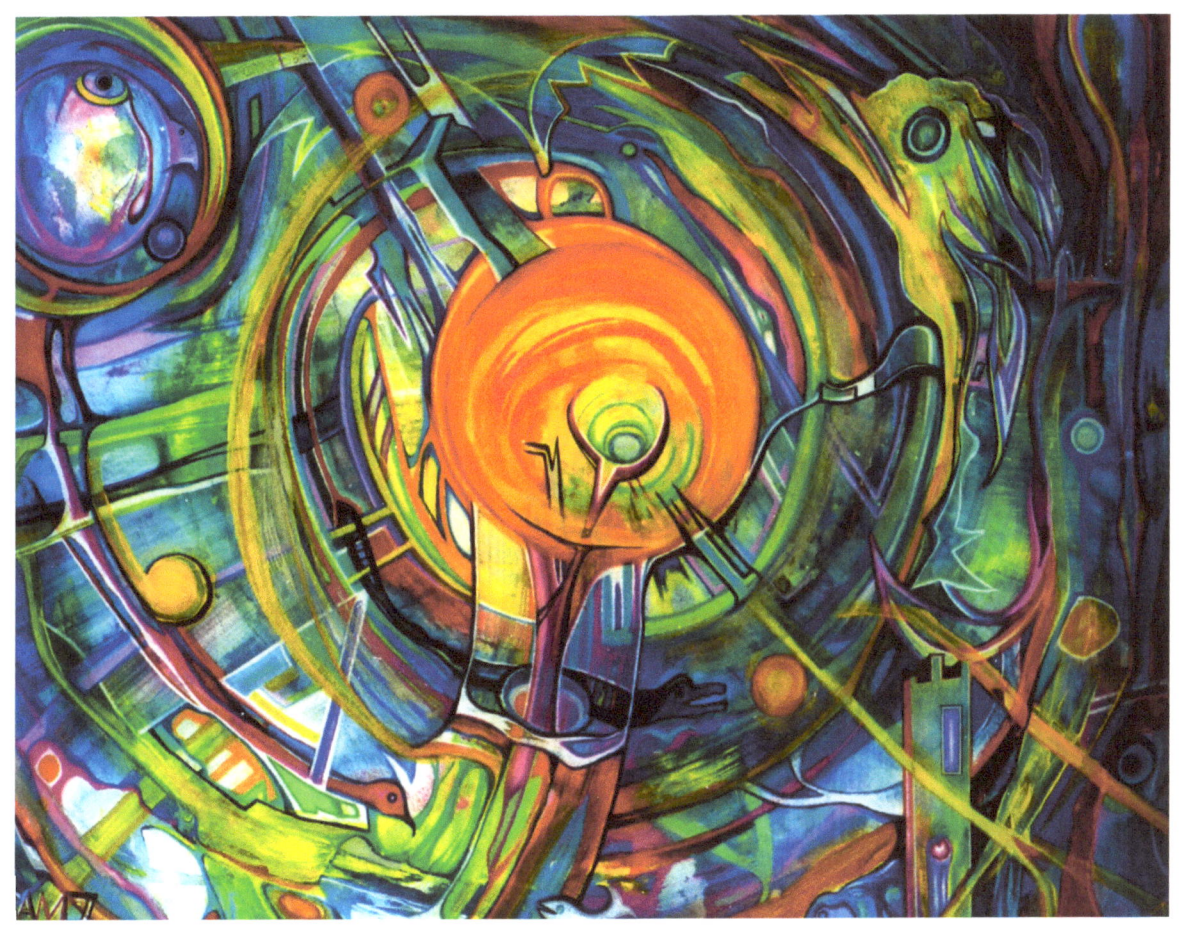

Other Worlds

About the Author

I am a self-taught artist. I started drawing and painting at age 14 to cope with my parents' divorce. At age 17, in 1973, I was diagnosed "manic-depressive." When I was 30, I had been thru 8 complete cycles (from depression, to brief stability, to mania -then psychosis). Despite these cycles, I had earned my bachelor's degree and continued to create art.

While psychotic I became very delusional and my "intact delusions" were very real to me and very urgent. There came a time that I realized that if I was going to stay alive and get off this sick rollercoaster, I had to decide if I was going to be fat & sane OR skinny & dead. I chose the first...and started taking Lithium.

My miracle med. I had 25 years of staying out of the hospital, working as a Mental Health Worker, then became extremely creative. ART saved my LIFE. Prior to the emergence of my current style in 1990, which I describe as "SURREAL-EXPRESSIVE," I had a very realistic style and would draw animals and people. I started experimenting with universal symbols and using art to express emotions in the summer of 1990. I realized that I could use my art to heal myself in a way that "talk therapy" could not. I became immersed in the creative process as memories surfaced and conflicts emerged in my art.

I noticed that I was in fact an "ARTIST," but was more involved in the healing process that was taking place. As a result of my personal journey, I now strongly believe in the HEALING POWER of ART. I also believe that I was meant to be an artist and that I need to create in order to be happy. I have been prolific since 1990, and find that since I have worked through a lot of my personal pain, I am now able to create new worlds and have fun with my art.

My health continues to be a challenge. I found out that I had diabetes in 1989, and stopped smoking and drinking. In 1998, I found out I had kidney disease caused by the 25 years of lithium and stopped taking it. I was not ever "right" for the next 5 years until I had 2 more severe episodes on the wrong meds and had been rapid cycling when they started me back with the lithium. It almost immediately brought me back to stable/normal.

I am not saying there is a right or wrong decision when one is faced with this dilemma... This is what I went thru. I can't speak for others - my case was/is "extreme." I guess you have to weigh the benefits with the side effects. I am still alive and stable - and happy, creative, and yes overweight. I watch myself, see my psychiatrist, and take my meds. I am doing everything I can to stop another manic episode from disrupting my life.

I want to encourage those who live with a mental illness to Lift UP your Positive, Tell Your Story, & Educate the Public. Together, we can remove the Stigma against mental illness.

SylviAnn Murray, 2014

www.ingramcontent.com/pod-product-compliance
Lightning Source LLC
Chambersburg PA
CBHW050745180526
45159CB00003B/1358